New Orientations in the Teaching of English

New Orientations
in the Teaching of English

Peter Strevens

Oxford University Press
1977

Oxford University Press, Walton Street, Oxford OX2 6DP

OXFORD LONDON GLASGOW NEW YORK TORONTO
MELBOURNE WELLINGTON CAPE TOWN IBADAN NAIROBI
DAR ES SALAAM LUSAKA KUALA LUMPUR
SINGAPORE JAKARTA HONG KONG TOKYO DELHI
BOMBAY CALCUTTA MADRAS KARACHI

ISBN 0 19 437076 3

Printed and bound in Great Britain by
Morrison & Gibb Ltd, London and Edinburgh

To Gwyn

Acknowledgements

For most of the period during which the chapters of this book (or the papers on which they are based) were being prepared, I have been engaged in teaching undergraduate and postgraduate students from many parts of the world, in helping to train and re-train teachers, in paying longer or shorter visits to fellow-professionals in a large number of foreign countries. It is from them, my students and colleagues, that I have gained most of my ideas. To all of them, especially to colleagues and postgraduate students at the Universities of Edinburgh, Leeds and Essex, at the Linguistic Society of America's Summer Institute held in UCLA in 1966, at the Regional English Language Centre, Singapore, at the Culture Learning Institute of the East-West Center in Hawaii, at the Linguistics Institute of the University of Cairo, and at the TESL Centre of Concordia University, Montreal, I acknowledge deep personal and professional debts.

I have already mentioned my gratitude to the great body of friends—students and colleagues—who are the main source of my thinking and who have had to sit through the many courses of lectures, seminars and presentations out of which most of the chapters in this book were fashioned. But preparing lectures, polishing and presenting papers at conferences often thousands of miles from home, writing and revising chapters of a book—all these are tasks which overlay into private life and interfere with family time and privacy. So this book is dedicated to my wife who has for so long cheerfully put up with absences and over-time, and whose support, though publicly usually invisible, is essential, and makes a book like this possible.

Peter Strevens
Wolfson College
Cambridge
1976

Acknowledgements are made to the following publishers from whose texts earlier versions of these papers have been taken:
The American Academy of Arts and Sciences, Harvard University, for

viii   Acknowledgements

'Second language learning' (here revised) which appeared in an earlier form in *Daedalus*, summer 1973.

The Ontario Institute for Studies in Education (Toronto), for 'A theoretical model of the language learning/teaching process' which appeared in the *Working Papers on Bilingualism/Travaux de recherches sur le bilinguisme*, Number 11, August 1976.

AILA Conference Proceedings, for 'On defining applied linguistics', which appeared in the *Proceedings of the Fourth International Congress of Applied Linguistics*, Volume 1, 1976, HochschulVerlag, Stuttgart.

Teachers of English to Speakers of Other Languages, for 'British and American methodology in English language teaching: similarities and differences' (here revised) which appeared in an earlier form in *ON TESOL 74*, Washington D. C., 1975.

Oxford University Press, for 'Some basic principles of teacher training' which appeared in the *English Language Teaching Journal*, Volume XXIX, No. 1, October 1974.

Oxford University Press, for 'Teaching the spoken language: phonetics, speech training and pronunciation teaching' (here revised) which appeared in an earlier form as 'A rationale for teaching pronunciation: the rival virtues of innocence and sophistication' in the *English Language Teaching Journal*, Volume XXVIII, No. 3, April 1974.

The Encyclopedia of Education, Lee C. Deighton, Editor-in-chief, Volume 3, for 'British and American English' (here revised). Copyright © Crowell-Collier Educational Corporation, 1971.

Université de l'État à Mons, Belgium, for 'Advantages and limitations of the language laboratory' (here revised) which appeared in an earlier form as 'Some observations on language labs' in *Revue de Phonétique Appliquée*, No. 5, 1967.

Cambridge University Press, for 'Where has all the money gone? The need for cost-effectiveness studies in the teaching of foreign languages' which appeared in *Applications of Linguistics. Selected Papers of the Second International Congress of Applied Linguistics, Cambridge 1969*, G. Perren and J. L. Trim (eds.), 1971.

Contents

Introduction

In the past decade there have emerged a number of important issues and concerns in applied linguistics, language-teaching methodology and the teaching of English, whose combined effect has been to open new paths of thought, action and development in the teaching of English. These new paths can be seen in studies of the philosophical and theoretical bases of language learning and language teaching; in fresh approaches to methodology and techniques of presentation; in the readiness of teachers to offer special solutions to new needs and demands; in new and illuminating studies of particular languages, especially of present-day English; in the application to language teaching of equipment and techniques whenever these seem appropriate. The five parts into which this book is divided reflect these new orientations in the teaching of English.

The five main areas with which the book is concerned are these: Part One (*Principle and Theory in Language Teaching*) reflects the profession's recent concern with explanations, with acquiring a stronger intellectual base for its practical operations. In Chapter 1 this process is considered in relation to the decline of the audio-lingual method, and especially to the false assumption that a single 'best' method might exist which would be suitable for all circumstances and all learners. Chapter 2 outlines a theoretical model of the language learning-teaching process, suggesting that all the vast complexity of language teaching and language learning can be accounted for, and hence better understood, if it is seen as a process in which a small number of variables interact with each other. Chapter 3 attempts a definition of 'applied linguistics' as a multi-disciplinary approach to any and all language-based problems, with language teaching prominent among these. In Chapter 4 the discussion is of similarities and differences between the acquisition of the mother tongue and the learning (with a teacher) of a subsequent language; in this chapter there is a detailed analysis of the many qualities which the learner and the teacher bring to their mutual interaction.

Part Two (*Methodology and Teacher Training*) contains three chapters.

Chapter 5 discusses similarities and differences between British and American approaches to ELT, and contains a detailed description of current British practice and methodology. Chapter 6 presents a statement of basic principles which determine the training of teachers of a foreign language, while Chapter 7 is concerned with a rationale for the teaching of the spoken language.

In Part Three, two *Special Problems in ELT* are selected for discussion. Chapter 8 offers a major analysis of the fast-growing subject of English for Special Purposes (ESP) and gives an extensive listing of the categories of communicative needs of one kind of learner. The theme of Chapter 9 is the learning and teaching of reading, with which is linked a tentative definition of what we mean by the terms *beginner*, *intermediate* and *advanced*.

Part Four is entitled *The Language We Teach*. Two of its chapters, 10 and 11, look in different ways at the question of the many varieties of English, and offer detailed frameworks for describing them. In Chapter 12 the theme is a brief contrastive description of British and American English.

Part Five (*Some Technical Questions*) deals, in Chapter 13, with language laboratories, presenting an explanation for the extraordinary polarization that occurs between on the one hand those for whom the language lab is a source of success and encouragement, and on the other those for whom it is a sham and a deception; and listing the minimum requirements for using a language lab with success. Chapter 14 looks at the need for our profession to be aware of the large amounts of money it spends and to know that techniques exist for finding out the value of much of our expenditure.

Part One

Principle and Theory in Language Teaching

1 Second language learning

Perhaps 250 million people alive today have received instruction in at least one foreign language. Yet, unlike the scientific disciplines of linguistics and psychology with which it has been linked in the past two decades, language teaching has remained an art and a craft whose theoretical and philosophical foundations are only now being elaborated. The average rate of success in learning a foreign language achieved by learners today is probably much higher than that of their parents; still, language teachers continue to seek means to improve the ease and effectiveness of language learning, through modifications in their ways of teaching.

In spite of the seminal work of Henry Sweet, Otto Jespersen, Harold Palmer and others, there is no accepted, well-articulated theory taking account of all the complex elements entailed in the organized teaching and learning of languages; the history of language teaching during the past fifty years describes, chiefly, a search for the single most effective 'method' of optimizing learning while standardizing and, hopefully, minimizing teaching, together with a quantity of experimentation whose results have often been ambiguous or too specific to lend themselves to generalization.

In the 1920's, the *direct method* sought to replace the classical, literature-based *grammar-translation method*; it advocated learning by hearing the language spoken, forbidding all use of the learner's native language in class; in the 1930's, strict control of the vocabulary and grammatical structures presented sought to systematize the work of the teacher and to provide principles for feeding the learner with an input designed to match his presumed learning tactics; in the 1940's, the U.S. Army Specialized Teaching Program (ASTP) and its counterpart in Britain incorporated some of the ideas of Bloomfieldian and European descriptive linguistics respectively, into intensive specialized courses for teaching languages to service personnel by *audio-lingual methods*; in the 1950's, in the United States, the audio-lingual method was consciously developed on the theoretical bases of the findings of Bloomfieldian structuralist linguistics and of behaviourist psychology, while in France a composite *audio-visual method* was elaborated, using integrated texts, recordings and illustrations, and based on the teaching concepts of *psycho-pédagogie* rather than on linguistics, and in Britain (where teachers have been less eager than their American counterparts to justify their teaching procedures by reference to a theory) improvements in methodology largely consisted of techniques for teaching younger children in the school systems of developing countries; in the 1960's, American audio-lingual methods were expanded for use with younger learners, especially with those learning English as a foreign language overseas, and language teachers everywhere, affected at one remove by dramatic developments in theoretical linguistics and especially in psycholinguistics, began to question their principles and procedures, to express dissatisfaction with the shortcomings of language-teaching methods, and to seek new ways of improving their effectiveness.

In the quarter-century since 1950, during which language teaching has been dominated by linguistics, the belief in a unique, best method has perhaps been fed by the heated partisanship of the various schools of linguistics. All the more frustrating then is the inevitable discovery that a particular teaching method, though demonstrably used with spectacular success in one place, may give poor results in another.

Experimentation has also brought its disappointments. It may not seem difficult to design a range of critical experiments to compare the effectiveness of method X and method Y; equally, it may seem plausible that by such experiments the general or inherent superiority of method X or Y could be established. Alas, twenty-five years of such experiments reveal only the multiplicity of confounding variables and the astonishing particularity of such separate school, class, teacher, and learner. The lessons to be learned from research are clear and repeated: first, it is extremely difficult to design experiments in comparative methodology that are not falsified by unforeseen or fortuitous circumstances, and second, the great variability of learning-teaching situations may render the results of any single valid experiment only partially applicable to the precise conditions in which particular learners are working elsewhere.

Two kinds of effort, then, were devoted to the same end. One effort was methodological—or rather, to use a term which we shall use more precisely in Chapter 2, it was directed towards the elaboration of an *approach*, a 'package deal' of materials and methodology backed by a rationale intended to explain and justify the proposed methodology. The other effort was experimental—an attempt to use scientific procedures in order to be able to say 'This method of language teaching is better than that'.

Both these kinds of effort rest upon a pair of assumptions which were not stated or argued: first, that language learning is sufficiently homogeneous for a single method to fit all circumstances; and second, that the achievement of relative success or failure in language learning is to be ascribed, above all, to method, and not significantly to other factors.

Both these assumptions are probably false. In the first place, the complex circumstances of teaching and learning languages—with different kinds of pupils, teachers, aims and objectives, approaches, methods and materials, classroom techniques, and standards of achievement—make it inconceivable that any single method could achieve optimum success in all circumstances. Indeed, as we shall see in the next chapter, there are so many factors in the achievement of success— and method is only one of them—that there is no reason to suppose that any single factor is solely or even largely responsible for success, still less that method is such a factor. As H. H. Stern points out:

we cannot say that we have found as yet a completely satisfactory solution to the basic difficulties of second-language learning. The primary weakness . . . lies in the *search for single or restricted solutions of major problems*. . . . Language teaching . . . suffers from oversimplification and primitivism.
(*Perspectives on Second Language Teaching*)

The most recent 'method' to gain a following is that of *cognitive-code* learning and teaching.

According to this theory, learning a language is a process of acquiring conscious control of the phonological, grammatical and lexical patterns of a second language, largely through study and analysis of these patterns as a body of knowledge. . . . Provided the student has a proper degree of cognitive control over the structures of the language, facility will develop utomatically with the use of the language in meaningful situations.
(J. B. Carroll, 'The Contribution of Psychological Theory and Educational Research to the Teaching of Foreign Languages')

There is no doubt that this approach, concentrating as it does on the learner's processes of knowing rather than on mechanistic procedures imposed upon him by the teacher, is in keeping with the anti-authoritarian, learner-centred educational outlook which is sweeping through much of the world and which we shall return to in later chapters. At the level of psychological learning theory, the *cognitive-code* method signals a rejection of stimulus-response models; at the level of linguistic theory, it signals rejection of the view that language is external to the mind of the individual; and at the level of teaching techniques, it signals the encouragement of deliberate grammar teaching as an aid to learning.

Herein lies an illustration of the fallacy of trying to find a unique methodological approach. In the audio-lingual method, teachers were warned *not* to tell the learner *about* the language—roughly speaking, not to teach them grammar. This was a general interdiction intended to apply to all learners since it is based on principle and theory. In the cognitive-code method, teachers are *required* to tell the learner *about* the language, and this too is a general, theory-based proposition. The fallacy is in the presupposition that one prescription must be right for the generality of learners, and the other false. In fact, it is the common experience of teachers that some kinds of learners are indeed helped by overt knowledge about the language they are learning (especially sophisticated adults with much previous foreign language learning experience) but that others are impeded by such techniques (especially young children).

One can argue, then, that the idea of a single 'best' method is intuitively unsatisfactory, that methodologies derived from theoretical linguistics or psychology alone may lead to contradictory classroom instructions, that the learning and teaching of languages is an activity requiring to be analysed in its own terms rather than solely in terms of other disciplines, even when these disciplines are obviously related in some fairly close way to the learning and teaching of languages. Such arguments lead one to be sceptical of dogma in language teaching and to seek other orientations for the process of learning-while-being-taught, which language teachers are attempting to encourage and promote.

However, it is a long step from rejection of commonly-held professional beliefs to the construction of a framework of propositions that hangs together logically and rationally, fits in with one's subjective assessment of how language teaching works, and squares with the facts as far as one can observe and discover them in the mind-bending complexity of present-day language teaching. Yet it is just such a step that is called for in developing a theory of language teaching which will be different from and not dependent upon theories of linguistics or psychology. In Chapter 2 we shall describe a theory of this kind: in the remaining sections of this chapter we shall illustrate two of the several stages which lead from simple rejection of the idea that there must be a 'best method' for all circumstances, towards a position where one can say 'In these particular learning/teaching circumstances we may reasonably predict that the most effective kind of learning may be promoted by the following kinds of teaching.'

Suppose that one doubts the truth of the claim that any one method is equally appropriate for all learners and all circumstances. Are there in the shared experience of language teachers some observations that might support one's scepticism and at the same time suggest a way towards a different solution? It seems to me that there are such observations and that as one considers them in detail they begin to display patterns of similarity and to arrange themselves in related sets.

To take a first example, it is a common observation, so obvious and well-known that at first sight it is almost trivial, that the kind of teaching which is appropriate to a young child is different from the kind of teaching that is most helpful to an adult learner. The reason why the kinds of teaching appropriate in the two cases are different from each other is that these categories of human beings approach the task of learning a language with a teacher in different ways. The young child's learning, and the teaching which most effectively stimulates and promotes it, is different from the adult's learning and the teaching most appropriate to him. What we are doing is to identify *pupil age* as a factor which reflects in the nature both of the learning and of the teaching best suited thereto. Having identified age as a variable we can go further and suggest that in addition to a difference between the young child and the adult we can also discern a difference between either of these age-groups and the adolescent.

Of course, it is not being suggested here that there are no similarities between the way individuals learn languages at various stages in their lifetime. On the contrary, as we shall see when we consider in the next chapter the factors which every human individual brings to the task of learning a language, there are indeed some universal similarities, regardless of age. At the same time the common experience of teachers is that there are differences, too, and it is these differences that are identified along the dimension of pupil age.

Another illustration concerns the educational framework within which the learning and teaching are embedded. Even taking learners of the same age-group it turns out that the learner whose language course is part of a general education of the usual kind, oriented towards literature, is engaged in a different task from the learner whose language course has no deliberate cultural affinities and is (for example) aimed at achieving a practical command of particular language 'skills' for use in a given occupation—in short, English as a Liberal Arts subject presents a different task to learner and teacher alike from English for reading engineering manuals for the maintenance of aircraft engines. It is not only a difference of content: the learner is working towards different communicative objectives; his learning has a different intellectual orientation—and the teaching has to reflect these and other differences. Here is a second example of differences of language learning/teaching type to set beside the differences of pupil age.

Even the learner's progress from zero command of the foreign language throughout his personal history of improvement up to the apex of his learning (however advanced or lowly that may be) is certain to entail changes in the way he learns and therefore in the most effective way of teaching him. The 'beginner', the 'intermediate' and the 'advanced' learner require distinct and different kinds of help from a teacher. But for the present we simply observe the existence of these distinctions as an illustration of another way in which learning and teaching vary along a particular dimension.

The three examples we have outlined thus far—pupil age, educational framework, stage of proficiency—are of roughly the same kind, and they seem to be allied to others which we shall consider in the next chapter, so that they can be regarded as forming a set, which we shall call 'language learning/teaching types'. But they are different in kind from another group of factors commonly observed to influence learning and teaching.

In this second set of variables we can notice, for instance, the quantity and intensity of instruction. Without embarking at this point upon the detailed discussion which follows in the next chapter, we can nevertheless observe that undergoing sufficient instruction to reach a given criterion, or insufficient instruction—or even too much instruction—are all considerations of importance. So, too, is the intensity of the learning and teaching (e.g. how many hours per week). Not unlike these two as a possible constraint upon the achievement of learning is the existence of a number of physical and psychological impediments to teaching—such as overcrowding, noise, fatigue, etc. This leads us to seek a place in the total scheme for such constraints, as well as others, so that their contribution to success or failure is distinct from the contribution of methodology or indeed any other variable.

The foregoing is simply a sketch of the gradual process by which there is built up a picture of the whole process of learning and teaching languages, broken down into its 'elements', consisting of different sets of phenomena having different functions in the complex total. We shall pursue this kind of analysis and develop the ensuing synthesis into a model of the whole, in Chapter 2. For the moment, however, we should notice not simply that the apparent complexity of learning and teaching languages can be reduced to an orderly pattern, but also that in order to achieve this result we are driven to recognize both different kinds of learning and a number of other variables over and beyond 'method' which have important effects upon the degree of achievement of the learner. In so doing we confirm the statement made earlier that 'method' is far from being the only factor of importance, and we also find support for the view that no single method could be the most effective one for all learning/teaching situations.

Further confirmation of this view can be seen in the history of the 'audio-lingual method'. This term refers to a combination of teaching materials constructed according to a well-known specification, a fairly standard syllabus, and a rationale based on Bloomfieldian structural linguistics and Skinnerian behaviourist psychology.

This approach was dominant in the United States for over twenty years, but has now been demoted, even discredited. As far as the argument of this chapter is concerned, what is interesting is that the method was proposed and accepted as the 'best' method specifically because it was based on linguistics and on psychology (actually, on a particular school of thought in each case). And indeed the great success which the method enjoyed in the circumstances for which it was designed led many people to accept the claims of its rationale as having been confirmed by the results.

What were the circumstances for which the audio-lingual method was designed? They were these: the learners were mostly young adults seeking entry to American universities, and thus were highly selected for ability and very strongly motivated; the teachers were of high calibre, being for the most part native speakers of English and university teachers; the teaching was rather intensive; the learning and teaching took place in an English-speaking country. It would be unfair to a highly professional programme to suggest that in such conditions *any* method and materials would have a good chance of success. Nevertheless, it has to be acknowledged that the circumstances were basically favourable to successful learning. A great deal of success was achieved, and is still achieved, with methods of this kind in circumstances such as those outlined above.

In the wake of this success (and also, it must be said, often in a spirit of professional evangelism, an enthusiasm to show others how to achieve success in language teaching and learning by employing this method) audio-lingual methods were exported to a number of overseas countries, particularly to developing countries where English is taught and learned as a foreign language. More important still, these methods were introduced into the school systems, as distinct from the colleges and universities, of these countries. Although a great effort in training and re-training teachers to use these methods was carried out side-by-side with a degree of adaptation of audio-lingual materials to younger age-groups, most of the projects of this type achieved much less success than was predicted and hoped for.

Why should this be so? One answer that has been suggested is that the bases in linguistics and psychology were from the wrong stable, and that the substitution of Chomskyan transformational-generative theory and generative psycholinguistics for Bloomfieldian structuralism and Skinnerian conditioning theory would restore to audio-lingual teaching its status of 'best' method. It is not explained by those who propose this solution how or why a change from a base in one linguistic theory to a base in another will improve the success of the method in those circumstances where it has previously been unsuccessful, while continuing to be as successful as before in those circumstances where it was so. That is not to say that the linguistics and psychology associated with the name of Chomsky are not of great importance and value: of course they are. But that does not mean that they provide the solution to all ills. The underlying hypothesis beneath this suggestion of improving results by changing only the linguistic base is the same as that which lay below the original design of the audio-lingual approach, namely, that the superiority of a teaching method depends on its being founded in linguistics, and in a particular school of linguistics at that. This strikes me as flying in the face of experience.

Another hypothesis, much more likely, is that the lack of success achieved by means of audio-lingual teaching when it was exported to different conditions is that the method was not designed to fit those conditions, and that no amount of change in the linguistics can make up for this lack of suitability. What are the conditions we are talking about? First, the learners are adolescents or younger children; they are unselected as to ability; they are unmotivated towards learning English and sometimes even hostile towards doing so; the teaching is far from intensive, being spread thinly over a number of years; the teaching is provided by non-native speakers of English, often with insufficient professional training and a shaky command of the language they are teaching; and the whole process takes place not in an English-speaking environment but in a country where opportunities for hearing or experiencing English outside the classroom may be very few. Under these circumstances it is difficult to achieve success with *any* method, but the audio-lingual method contains some technical features that render it particularly unlikely to succeed.

This brief analysis of reasons for the success of the audio-lingual method in one set of conditions and not in another echoes one of the main themes of this book and reflects a view which is widely held among language teachers. This view is that the learning and teaching process is governed by a complex set of variables which we are at last beginning to identify and understand.

In later chapters we shall describe in greater detail what these variables are, and how they interact so as to make possible the achievement of greater or less success. However, before examining these factors and their contribution to success or failure, we need to ask, success or failure in relation to what? The term *success* is relative: it has to be considered in relation to the *aims* of the teaching and the learning. It ought to go without saying that the aims of language teaching in any particular case should be adequately stated, relevant to the learner, and realistic in the practical situation where learner and teacher come together. Unfortunately this is by no means always the case. There are many parts of the world where inadequate results can be traced, in part, to aims that are unrealistic, incoherent or contradictory. Even in the relatively sophisticated school systems of North America and Europe, *de facto* changes in the aims of language learning brought about by the evolution of social needs or of public opinion have not always been recognized in the stated aims of teaching.

Furthermore, the choice of which variety of a foreign language it is proper to teach is no longer always self-evident, being much influenced by the growth of national, ethnic and regional feelings of identity. The British have long accepted that in teaching English overseas there are some areas where it is appropriate to set the goal of speaking English like an Englishman (or an American), but that elsewhere such a goal is unacceptable and must be modified in the direction of, for example, speaking educated West African English. The French-Canadian learning English expects to speak Canadian English; but does the English-speaking Canadian learning French expect to speak Canadian French? What of relations between Black English and Standard American English? Is it reasonable for the black American to be expected to learn Standard English as a second dialect, or should white Americans accept the co-existence of a different dialect in their society? The days are long past when learning a particular language obviously and unequivocally meant learning a single, universally acknowledged standard form. Nowadays the precise aims and goals of language learning need to be in line with public needs, and revised as these needs change.

In conclusion, then, what are the salient features of second language learning as we approach the last quarter of the century? First, it is moving away from teacher-centred, creativity-engendering, custom-designed approaches. Second, teachers are abandoning overly simplistic ideas about teaching and learning, including the fallacy of the unique preferred methodology, in favour of a more difficult and complex but more realistic outlook based on analysing the dimensions of the learning situation for each set of learners. Third, it is becoming possible to identify the factors that maximize success and minimize failure so that those responsible for the organization of teaching can, by conscious acts, improve its effectiveness. Fourth, after a period of close dependence on linguistics and psycholinguistics, when it seemed to many that these disciplines could, between them, generate all the effective learning of languages that men might desire, the profession is engaged afresh, with improved intellectual tools, in increasing its understanding of the nature of teaching. Having avoided domination by the useful but essentially trivial assistance provided by technology in such forms as recording devices, language labs, and teaching machines, second language learning now emerges as a process and a task which for its further improvement requires an ever-deepening knowledge of its three equipollent elements: the mind of the learner, the nature of language, and the skill of the teacher.

2 A theoretical model of the language learning/teaching process

1. Introduction: Language Teaching and Theory

In this chapter we take up the question of theoretical studies in language teaching which was raised in Chapter 1. First we shall give some reasons why such studies are particularly needed at the present time; then we shall outline one possible model.

For two decades, language teachers have had their profession 'put down', either by implication or directly, through invidious comparisons with linguistics and psychology, disciplines which have undergone intense theoretical ferment during the same period; in consequence, language teachers have often been made to feel inferior to linguists and cognitive psychologists.

Within the past two or three years, however, a number of scholars have taken up the study of language teaching in general and abstract terms, working towards a general theory of language teaching in its own right, making use of insights from linguistics and psychology when they are relevant yet retaining as their central focus the unique and complex set of events which take place when a learner learns a language through the mediation of a teacher.

Of course, many scholars in the past sixty years or even longer have written about language teaching in terms of principle and theory. Current work must take account of Sweet, Jespersen, Palmer, West and Hornby; of Lado, Marckwardt and Fries; of Mackey, Rivers, Jakobovits, Wardhaugh, Valette and Disick; of Corder, Trim, Roulet, Candlin and Wilkins; of Dykstra and Johnson, Stern and Spolsky—and many others. But the reference here is to a new and accelerating effort, namely the attempt to understand the task or process as a whole, and to devise a theoretical model that fits its complexity. Perhaps W. F. Mackey's important *Language Teaching Analysis* was the work which laid the foundation for current studies by exposing for the first time in a comprehensive way the nature and the complexity of the language learning and teaching process.

It is necessary to refute the imputation that language teaching is an inferior occupation. On the contrary, language teaching is a task in which intelligence, imagination, training, command of language, experience, a body of knowledge and the exercise of judgment and compassion are essential qualities, and in which high standards are imposed and maintained, on a world-wide basis, by a particular branch of the profession of education. Becoming a teacher with high professional standards is different in its content and aims from becoming a good surgeon, or linguist, or lawyer, or psychologist; but it is similar in its reliance upon selective entry, special training, the attainment of skill before acceptance. Just as it is possible, and necessary, to distinguish between the untrained amateur medical doctor and the professional, so equally it is possible and necessary to distinguish between the untrained amateur language teacher and the professional.

Starting from the assumption then, that language teaching is one among a number of professions of equal value, the aim of this chapter is to outline one approach to the theoretical study of its operation. Specifically, the chapter proposes the minimum elements for a theory of the language learning/teaching process. That is to say, it suggests that the learning and teaching of languages can be viewed as a process; that the complexity of the process can be reduced to a minimum number of abstract elements; and that the inter-relationships between these elements can be shown in such a manner that any activity by any learner or teacher, as long as it is relevant to the learning and/or teaching of a language, can be assigned to some element of the theory and can be conceived in relation to the process as a whole.

2. Studies of What?

One feature of this theoretical approach is that it takes as its focus all those circumstances where a learner learns and a professional teacher teaches. It says nothing about learning a language by picking it up from living in a foreign country, nor about the way in which an infant acquires his first command of language. For the purposes of this chapter, the term *acquisition* will be taken to mean learning a language without benefit of a teacher and *learning* will be taken to mean learning with a teacher (and it should be remembered that the adult who works on his own with a self-study course is still, though in an extended way, learning with a teacher).

So we are concerned with what we shall call the language learning/ language teaching complex (abbreviated LL/LT): i.e., not just with learning, and not just with teaching, but with both. But this complex is also to be regarded as a *process*, that is, a series of events in which something is changed, and in which a particular condition at the start of the activity is gradually replaced by a sequence of other conditions tending more and more towards the desired final state. The LL/LT process is not instantaneous: it takes time. It is not accidental, it is deliberate: learner and teacher combine in seeking to reach a particular end-condition.

It is a characteristic of the profession of language teaching that it deals with an indefinitely large range of different learners, different teaching/learning conditions, different aims, etc. Yet in another sense LL/LT is concerned with a single individual learner and with his unique personal abilities and qualities, and with an individual teacher, and with a particular, unique set of surrounding circumstances. What the theoretical study must do is to provide a comprehensive way of understanding, at one and the same time, both the complete range of features which at once embrace and distinguish between *all* learners and teachers, and on the other hand the particular features possessed by any specific learner and teacher.

3. Elements of the LL/LT Process

Seen as a process, LL/LT turns out to have a beginning and an end, and to be promoted and impelled by particular *elements*. Table 1 lists the twelve essential elements of the LL/LT process.

TABLE 1: Elements of the LL/LT process

1. Policy and Aims
2. Administration and Organization
3. Relevant Professional Disciplines
4. Choice of LL/LT Types
5. Teacher Training
6. Approach
7. Pedagogy, Methodology, Instruction, Teaching
8. Syllabus Design
9. Materials Construction
10. Constraints on LL/LT Achievement
11. The Learner
12. Evaluation

The entries in Table 1 are simply labels: we shall discuss each element briefly before returning to the process as a whole, when we shall offer a diagram showing the interrelationships between the elements of this theoretical model.

4. Outline of the Elements of the LL/LT Process

Element 1: POLICY AND AIMS

This element reflects the public will, the social sanction for the organized provision of language instruction, the response to the linguistic needs of the community. This is the element which takes account of the fact that different communities make very different decisions about languages: some make little or no gesture towards the inclusion of foreign language teaching in their educational system; others build it in from the beginning of primary education; some even use a foreign language (e.g., English or French) as the medium of instruction in much or all of the school system. This element is where the sociolinguistic facts of a community—the languages its citizens speak, encounter, need to use, value highly (or value low), feel nostalgic about, regard as social and psychological symbols, etc.—find their general expression, and where this general expression is to some extent refined into opinions about how many of the population should be encouraged to reach what kind and level of proficiency in which languages. In a sense, this element provides much of the essential 'motive power' for the entire process, since in the absence of a public will that some members of the community should learn a particular language, that particular language will not be learned, at least not as a concerted and organized process. Examples of the workings of this element abound: in the United States, after the launching of the first Russian satellite, the country reacted by deciding that more Americans needed to have a better command of more languages, including Russian; in Britain, social changes led in the 1960's to a public feeling that most young children ought to be given a practical command of French; in Malaysia, the advent of independence was accompanied by a socio-political decision to promote and develop Bahasa Malaysia as the principal national language; there are many other examples.

PoLICY AND AIMS, then, is a label which refers to the public will that the sociolinguistic circumstances of the community shall be recognized by the provision of teaching facilities for learning languages.

Element 2: *ADMINISTRATION AND ORGANIZATION*

Once the public will is expressed, it has to be put into practice. This second element consists of the financial and administrative provision for language teaching in the schools and colleges, for training and paying teachers, for building or enlarging schools, for providing books and equipment, for running public examinations (but see element 12, EVALUATION), for organizing an inspectorate, for research and development. Ideally, this element is quickly responsive to major changes in POLICY AND AIMS; in some countries POLICY AND AIMS may even be formed, led and influenced by the senior administrators and specialists who operate the machinery of ADMINISTRATION AND ORGANIZATION. Elsewhere, particularly in developing countries with little money and great social problems, this second element may be inadequately financed and poorly organized.

This second element provides the financial and organizational framework and impetus to carry out the social decisions of the first element.

Element 3: RELEVANT PROFESSIONAL DISCIPLINES

The administrators (operating element 2) who put into operation the public will (expressed in element 1) serve a body of teachers in their country who have access to a vast international array of professional knowledge and experience, which in turn has some of its roots in major autonomous disciplines such as *education, linguistics, psychology, social theory*; and in the recently developed disciplines such as *sociolinguistics* and *psycholinguistics*. The importance of this third element of the model is its acknowledgment that the profession of language teaching, as administratively engendered by element 2, can seek assistance from many intellectual sources, each with its own individual justification for existence, yet each with its relevance for, and contribution to, the learning and teaching of languages.

Notice that this formulation contains two central assumptions: (a) that the contributing disciplines have their own autonomous justification, which has nothing to do with language learning and teaching, and (b) that each provides a contribution, no more, to the study of language learning and language teaching. Hereby hangs a great and continuing controversy. On the one side of the debate are ranged those who believe that language teaching is necessarily and desirably dominated by linguistics, and that language teaching without reference to linguistic theory—whether in Bloomfieldian structuralist terms or transformational-generative terms or any other—cannot be fully effective; on the other side are those (myself among them) who believe that language learning and language teaching are activities in their own right, which can be illuminated by some particular insights from different areas of linguistic theory, but which in the last analysis are independent of both linguistics and psychology.

One solution to this apparent conflict of views over the theoretical bases of language teaching is offered by the concept of *applied linguistics* as an inter-disciplinary approach to the solution of all kinds of language-based problems. A more detailed discussion and description of applied linguistics forms the theme of Chapter 3: for the moment we shall simply observe that one major way in which the contribution of the relevant disciplines finds its way into the language teaching profession is through applied linguistics, which increasingly provides a ready-made 'package' combining on the one hand an understanding of the practical, pragmatic difficulties of the teacher and learner, and on the other the relevant insights of theory.

The organization of language teaching in any country takes place not in isolation there but within a well-developed profession whose intellectual and practical bases are firmly established, with an international network of communications and with the collaboration of a world-wide array of centres of excellence. By providing links to this profession and to these centres—which are generally but not exclusively located in or derived from colleges, universities and research institutes—this third element is contributing, as do elements 1 and 2, to the 'motive power' which sets the entire process in motion.

Element 4: CHOICE OF LL/LT TYPES
If the three preceding elements can be regarded as cumulatively developing an impetus—public will + finance and administrative apparatus + disciplinary knowledge and insights—the fourth element can be regarded as 'shaping' the impetus, and in discussing this element we shall look more closely at some of the factors that were touched on in Chapter 1

What is meant by 'LL/LT types'? Much of the discussion about language teaching treats the process of learning and the process of teaching as if each was a single, unchanging set of activities. But in practice every teacher knows that both learning and teaching are altered in important ways by different circumstances. It is the nature of these changes and the factors that principally determine them which this fourth element of our theoretical model seeks to describe. Six such factors are isolated, and two or three 'types' of learning/teaching situation are identified within each factor, as in the following summary:

(i) PUPIL AGE—(young child–adolescent–adult)
(ii) STAGE OF PROFICIENCY—(beginner–intermediate–advanced)
(iii) EDUCATIONAL AIMS—(general educational–practical command–special and vocational purposes)
(iv) LEARNER INVOLVEMENT—(volunteer–non-volunteer)
(v) LANGUAGE OF INSTRUCTION STATUS—(mother tongue–target language–other foreign language)
(vi) TARGET LANGUAGE STATUS—('foreign' language–'second' language)

Discussion of LL/LT Types
4 (i) *Pupil Age*—It is the universal experience of language teachers that young children (say, age 6–13) display different characteristics from older learners. They bring to language learning an *initial* enthusiasm and assumption of success; they tend to learn easily and unselfconsciously; they are inordinately cast down by failure and buoyed up by success; they have a short attention-span; they are quickly fatigued; they are easily bored and almost as easily re-animated; they mimic easily and make unfamiliar sounds with enjoyment and without embarrassment; they are relatively untroubled by making errors in public; they

cannot seriously see their learning in terms of eventual usefulness; they are deeply affected by their relations with their teacher; their self-esteem, and in consequence their expectation of personal success, is easily bruised; at their best they can be a joy to be with and teach, but at their worst they can become sullen non-learners; and so on. Adults display very different characteristics: their enthusiasm is tempered by their reasons for learning; they can make a conscious effort to put up with fatigue and boredom for the sake of an ultimate goal; they imitate sounds less well; they are inhibited from making errors in the presence of their peers; they have 'learned how to learn', and can employ techniques such as guessing and analogy more freely than the young child; they tend to intellectualize their learning; they are often hidebound by the methods according to which they were themselves taught when at school; they are a repository of myths and old wives' tales about foreign languages and the learning of them; they have deep-seated but often erroneous beliefs about their own ability or inability to learn a foreign language; at their best, they learn fast and accurately, but at their worst they can totally fail to make progress. Lying somewhere between these polarities, adolescents are part way between children and adults, but they also have special characteristics of their own: they are liable to sudden and irrational likes or dislikes of the teacher, which carry over into their learning; they may be easily triggered out of learning by the sight of a member of the opposite sex, or by casual mention of one of the current symbols—revolution, love, ecology, drugs, abortion, pollution, etc.—after which the resumption of learning may be long delayed. At their best, they can be the fastest learners and the most accurate performers of all, but at their worst they can be bloody-minded class-wreckers. As far as the present argument is concerned, the point being made is that the learner's age determines the type of learning that takes place and the teaching that is appropriate to that kind of learning, and that three main learning/teaching types need to be distinguished, corresponding broadly to *young children, adolescents* and *adults*.

4 (ii) *Stage of Proficiency Reached*—A further difference which takes place in the type of learning depends on the stage of proficiency that the learner has reached. At the outset, the learner is totally dependent on the teacher (or on that other embodiment of a teacher, the course-book). He understands only in fragments, guided from smaller fragments to larger by the teacher, until the mysterious moment when for the first time the learner understands or produces a whole utterance or sentence for himself. From this point onwards the learning, and the teacher's role in promoting it, undergoes a change. While the learner was a beginner, the teacher had first to draw him along through a series of prepared learning experiences. This stage of learning is

teacher-centred. Now the learner has started to produce and create in the language—not perfectly, and with many set-backs—and the teacher's task is to encourage him to do so increasingly, to steer him away from 'error' and mislearning, to provide him with new rules for constructing sentences, new vocabulary, new skills in communicating, new awareness of acceptability and usage and appropriateness. This stage of learning is a joint teacher-learner campaign, and learners in this stage are usually called 'intermediate'. In a final 'advanced' stage, the learning is largely learner-centred: the teacher's task is to supply the learner with great quantities of reading and listening experience, to monitor his practice in speaking and writing, to plug gaps in his learning, to 'stretch' his capacity for learning, to lead him towards that state in which the learner, as it is often expressed, 'comes to think in the foreign language'—to depend less and less on the mediation of his mother tongue. None of this is news to the experienced teacher. Its importance at this point is that it constitutes a further distinction between different types of learning, to which the teacher responds by a different type of teaching.

4 (iii) *Educational Aims*—This choice of LL/LT type reflects the main kinds of language teaching course that are offered. The conventional framework for language teaching, at least up to age 18, has been as *part of a general education*, in which the language has been an element in a cultural experience on the humanities side. (At one time it was also assumed that the ultimate use to be made of the language would be to study literature in the language concerned, but this aim is becoming rare except for university students of languages.) Teaching a language within a general educational framework inevitably gives to the teaching a particular 'colouring'; for younger learners it means that the language-learning experience is woven in with mental and emotional development. A second type of framework is the course where the aims are simply *to acquire maximum command of the language*, unrelated to other kinds of education or subject learning. In these circumstances the 'colouring' of the teaching is subtly different. Yet a third type is found where the language, or even just a restricted sub-set of the language, is learned *for special or vocational purposes*. The airline pilot or ground controller learning the international English of the air is a case in point; so is the Polish specialist in public health who learns English for work in India; or the Norwegian secretary who learns to handle office practice in English. This dimension of choice affects above all the teaching, and the learning only indirectly.

4 (iv) *Learner Involvement*—Teachers recognize a distinction between the learning that takes place (and the teaching that can be attempted) when the learner is learning because he has chosen to do so, and that which applies when the learner is learning without this degree of

involvement. This factor is frequently assigned to the catch-all label of Motivation, but it seems in fact to merit being included as one of the LL/LT types, since it directly affects the teaching and learning. The teacher can expect of the 'volunteer' learner an attitude towards learning and towards being taught which he cannot expect of the 'non-volunteer'. The volunteer accepts higher expectations for himself, puts up better with fatigue, resists boredom, needs less cajoling and fewer of the interest-arousing techniques of the teacher, and he usually learns at a rate closer to his personal maximum learning-rate than does the non-volunteer.

4 (v) *Language of Instruction Status*—The third choice of LL/LT type is one that is imposed from without, whereas in the two previous cases the change was internal to the learner. The learning task is different, especially in the beginner's and intermediate stages, depending on whether the instruction is couched in the learner's mother tongue, or in the target language itself, or in some other language. The commonest case is no doubt for the medium of instruction to be the learner's own mother tongue, which presents him with a known, sure reference base to which he can and often does refuge his mind if the learning gets tough. But a considerable amount of language instruction takes place in a presentational framework of the target language itself, for example, when English is the medium of instruction as well as the language being learned; or when some subjects on the curriculum, but not all, are taught in the foreign language. Here the learner has no easy refuge for his language-learning attention to flee to, and there is reason to believe that these circumstances (that is, when the language being learned is being used as the medium of instruction) can be manipulated so as to bring about proportionately more effective learning than the L1 situation. A different language framework occurs where an additional foreign language is learned through the medium of one learned previously: for example, when English is taught to Tunisians or Cambodians, not through Arabic or Khmer respectively, but through French. This particular set of choices of LL/LT type affects both the learning and the teaching.

4 (vi) *Target Language Status: 'foreign' or 'second' language*— The last of the LL/LT types we need to consider relates to the distinction between a *foreign* and a *second* language. The second language situation exists where the language has special status in the community (usually for historical reasons), as an official language in the courts, as the medium of instruction in some sectors of public education, as a *lingua franca*, etc. Under these circumstances there is normally a pervasive public awareness of the language (e.g. English or French), though the general standards of competence in it are not necessarily very high. When the language being learned is a *foreign*

language, no such favourable external circumstances exist, and the language is on a par with all others that are taught. The effect of this distinction upon teaching and learning is very considerable, in the attitudes of the learners and teachers towards their task, in the kinds of teaching techniques that are commonly successful, and in the average levels of achievement that are expected. The FL/SL distinction is a clear-cut example of a difference of language learning/language teaching type such as this fourth element of the model takes account of.

At this point in the description of the theoretical model we begin discussion of a complex set of activities which can be loosely grouped together under the label of 'teaching'. It will be necessary to distinguish between the following sub-divisions of the total set, each of which constitutes a separate element in the model: TEACHER TRAINING; APPROACH; PEDAGOGY, METHODOLOGY, INSTRUCTION, TEACHING; SYLLA- BUS DESIGN; MATERIALS DESIGN. One of these sub-divisions, TEACHER TRAINING, has functions beyond the obvious ones conveyed by its title: it is also the channel by which, in the long term, the aims of language teaching, its organization, and its links with the worldwide profession, are converted into classroom action of a particular kind. Equally, it is the principal channel through which changes and reforms in language teaching can be brought about. For these reasons we deal with it as the first of the five elements concerned with teaching. The subject of teacher training is taken up again and elaborated in more detail in Chapter 6. Here we simply outline its main factors and show how teacher training fits into the model as a whole.

Element 5: TEACHER TRAINING

The general effectiveness of language learning and teaching in any given country is heavily dependent on the nature and quality of the training which teachers undergo before entering their profession. Just as there is a great range of different kinds of learners, different aims, different standards of achievement, so there exists also a great range of different types of teacher training courses. Nevertheless, it is possible to attempt a set of generalizations which embody the essential variables. (We shall describe the basic principles in a way which relates particularly to *initial teacher training*; but similar aims underlie *in-service training* and other forms of *further training*, though action must be adapted to the different circumstances.)

Training a teacher entails the *selection* of potentially suitable indi- viduals (and by implication, the elimination of unsuitable applicants); the continuing *personal education* of the trainee so that the teacher can be seen to be a member of the educated sector of the community;

general training as a teacher irrespective of specialization; and *special training as a language teacher*. The concerted aim of these procedures is to bring each individual trainee as close as possible to the ideal, in which a teacher combines the necessary *personal qualities* (of intelligence, a 'non-discouraging' personality, emotional maturity, etc.) with a command of *technical skills* (in maximizing the learning of his pupils, controlling classroom activity, manipulating the teaching materials), and a humane *professional understanding* of his career and his educational role.

The training courses which lead towards the creation of the ideal teacher generally contain three different components: a *skills* component, an *information* component and a *theory* component. The *skills* component embraces the teacher's command of the language he is teaching, teaching techniques and classroom activities, including the 'management of learning', through which the teacher assesses the progress of each individual and adjusts his teaching accordingly. Training for these skills essentially requires great practice, in both simulated and genuine teaching situations, and careful analysis of the trainee's successes and failures. The *information* component includes information about education, about the syllabus he will be following and the materials he will be using, and about the nature of language. The *theory* component brings in an appropriate selection of the theoretical findings from educational philosophy, psychology, linguistics, applied linguistics, etc.

However, few teacher-training courses can be ideal. In particular, most courses have far too little time to put on a truly comprehensive training course, being subject to administrative and financial restrictions; many courses have to train applicants who are too young, or who have an inadequate level of personal education; sometimes the training institution lacks sufficient staff of the necessary standard, or lacks facilities, especially for supervised teaching practice. The teacher trainer faces a continual battle to achieve, in the short time at his disposal and given the standards of trainee and staff that he has available, the best possible mix of skills, information and theory.

Thus the teacher-training element of our model demonstrates an inherent characteristic of the whole LL/LT process: the teaching profession holds to an image of the ideal, in which a fully-trained teacher would assist a co-operative learner to achieve, at his maximum learning-rate, the closest approximation of native-speaker competence which is possible in the time; yet the ideal is in practice almost always flawed, so that the end-product falls short of the standard that the teacher believes might have been reached. But the ideal buoys up the teacher and encourages him to carry on, despite setbacks, year after year. It is a not negligible function of the teacher-training element of

LL/LT to inject into the whole process an enthusiasm, a sense of pride in achievement, a desire to go on improving the results attained by one's pupils, a personal energy and drive on the part of the teacher which will last throughout his or her career.

Element 6: APPROACH

By APPROACH is meant a commitment to particular, specified points of view—to an ideology, one might say—about language teaching. Adherence to the set of ideas which characterized the *audio-lingual method* is one example of an approach; adherence to *cognitive-code* teaching is another (as long as it rests on well-formulated propositions and is not simply a label saying 'I used to be an audio-lingual person but I gave it up'). Direct Method teaching embodied an approach; so did—and does—grammar-translation teaching.

There is much confusion over terms used in order to designate a 'package deal' of attitudes, theories, methods, techniques; in many cases the word 'Method' (as in 'Audio-Lingual Method') conveys just such a composite set of notions, and this is an Approach in the sense used here.

Approaches evolve as a consequence of the need to turn ideas for reform into a comprehensive drive for action. It is not sufficient to believe that levitation (let us say) is an important new factor whose use in appropriate ways would lead to significant improvements in the success of language learning and teaching. That alone would not merit being called an Approach. But if one were to persuade other teachers that one is right (by writing articles and books on the subject), and to produce teaching materials embodying the idea ('English through Levitation: a course for beginners'), and to train teachers in the use of these materials, and to publish the rationale and principles behind one's proposals ('Gravity and Language', 'Linguistics and Weightlessness', 'Theoretical Studies in Resisting the Pull of Gravity: their relevance to language teaching', etc.) then the whole package might be designated 'The Anti-Gravitational Approach: better language teaching through levitation'.

Many teachers teach and are trained outside the confines of any specific approach; others cut across the boundaries and teach in ways that relate partly to one approach and partly to another. This does not necessarily matter: no one approach has the monopoly of either success or failure.

Nevertheless, a few formulated approaches do exist and many teachers do follow one or another of them, so that it is necessary to make provision for APPROACH as an element in the theory, with the reservation that in addition to Approaches X, Y and Z, provision must be made in this element for the categories 'Don't know', 'Mixed' and 'Undefined'.

Element 7: PEDAGOGY, METHODOLOGY, INSTRUCTION, TEACHING

The reason for including four terms in the label of this element is that different authorities define these terms somewhat differently, and it is necessary to bring in most shades of most of the meanings. This element is concerned with the presentation to the learner of the material he is learning, with different techniques, tips, hints, gimmicks, systems, instructions, etc. for doing this, for organizing it, and for describing the process. It is the element that takes account of the full range of class-room (and non-classroom) presentations; of teaching games and entertainments; of drills and exercises; of the integration of prior 'softening-up' with initial presentation and subsequent consolidation and repetition; of the 'management of learning' by the teacher as he assesses the moment-to-moment progress of each learner and adjusts his teaching accordingly; of changes of pace; of ways to detect and overcome boredom; indeed, of all the possible deliberate activities that promote learning and defeat non-learning.

In one sense, this is the heart, and certainly the art, of teaching. It is the component which has been the most voluminously written about but the least analysed and systematized. It is the element where the directed intelligence of one human being, the teacher, interacts with and deliberately guides, the directed intelligence of another human being, the learner. In another sense, it is the element where practical group psychology is in action, where the single class teacher may be subjected to separate and concerted action by a group of people, in ways that may either promote the learning task ('Please sir, tell us about Paris'); or may be quite irrelevant to it ('Please miss, it's raining'); or may be inimical to it ('We're not interested: we want to play football').

PEDAGOGY, etc. includes not only conventional classroom techniques but also any specialized teaching techniques that may be developed for particular use: programmed instruction techniques, for example, language-lab techniques, individualization procedures, self-teaching methods, small group techniques for use in large classes, community language programmes, peer-group teaching—any and every means of deliberately achieving the learning of particular language material.

It must be realized that in identifying an element of the process as 'Pedagogy' we are absolutely not implying that existing techniques of teaching and learning must be retained, nor that any particular method-ology is better or worse than any other. Quite the reverse: it accords with the multiple, complex nature of language learning that language teaching should itself be diverse; and it accords with the changing nature of learners' aims and needs that language teaching should itself change. The professional task is not only to identify the learners' needs and to select the most appropriate kind of instruction taking all the conditions into account, but also to identify the shortcomings of teaching and to devise ways of overcoming them. This element, then, defines not only the existing range of teaching techniques but also methods still being conceived and others not yet dreamed of. It is open-ended and forward-looking, not closed and conservative.

Element 8: SYLLABUS DESIGN

The syllabus (U.S.: *curriculum*) is partly an administrative instrument, partly a day-to-day guide to the teacher, partly a statement of what is to be taught and how, sometimes partly a statement of an approach. It is the document in which is listed, ideally, the items to be taught, in a particular course, to a particular set of defined learners, on a given number of occasions per week or day, in a given sequence, with the aim of achieving stated interim and final goals or objectives, and (usually) according to particular teaching techniques for each and every item. The syllabus embodies that part of the language which is to be taught, broken down into 'items' or otherwise processed for teaching purposes.

The design of syllabuses is a task about which much has been written, especially in two respects: first, in discussion of *selection* and *grading* (i.e. the choice of items to be included and the ordering of those items in a particular sequence); and more recently, in considering the underlying bases of what it is that is being selected and graded.

An era of *linguistically-based syllabuses* (i.e. in which the teaching items were 'language items' from grammar, vocabulary, phonology) has been succeeded by an era of *situationally-based syllabuses* (i.e. in which topics, themes, situations are selected and graded first), and this may be followed by an era of *notional* or *semantic syllabuses*.

The suggestion for notional syllabuses forms part of the important work being produced by the team headed by J. L. M. Trim under the auspices of the Council of Europe. This group is preparing a rationale and a specification for materials to be used in teaching any of the languages of Europe to pre-determined levels of achievement, the learning and teaching stages to have equivalence across languages. (This is the 'unit-credit' system: see Van Ek, J., *The Threshold Level*.) Contributing to this work, David Wilkins has proposed (in *Notional Syllabuses: a contribution to foreign language curriculum development*) a fresh, additional criterion for syllabus design, in the form of a comprehensive set of 'notional' categories for inclusion in syllabuses. These are sub-divided into: (i) *semantico-grammatical categories*—expressing universal concepts of time, quantity, space and matter, as well as expressing grammatical concepts of *case* ('who did it, who it happened to, and what got changed') and *deixis* (categories of reference such as pronouns, demonstratives, anaphora, etc.); and (ii) *categories of communicative function*—expressing such qualities as *modality* (certainty, necessity, obligation . . .), *moral evaluation* (judgment, approval/disapproval . . .), *suasion, argument, enquiry, emotions*, and *interpersonal relations*. Notions, it will be seen, are a means of hooking the syllabus, as may be required, into the meaning of anything in the universe.

New developments in syllabus-construction are having the effect of (a) contributing to language teaching some insights from linguistics, psycholinguistics and sociolinguistics, and (b) broadening the profession's view of what should be taught and learned, for instance by acknowledging that communicative abilities form an important portion of the learning and teaching content. (Many teachers, citing Gouin and Comenius, will object that these abilities have been included for decades, if not for centuries; but the importance of the new breadth displayed in syllabus design is that it reverses an existing, fairly recent tendency to narrowness.)

It seems likely that syllabus design will shortly undergo a period of rapid development and systematization. For the moment, in addition to noting that this is an essential element in the total LL/LT process, we shall simply observe that any syllabus must be both *realistic* in terms of what the teachers and learners can actually achieve who are required to follow it and *relevant* to the aims and objectives of the public will—and it is unfortunately the case in some countries, particularly developing countries, that syllabuses have been designed according to modern professional thought and approaches derived from America or Europe, but have then been imposed without regard either to the relevance of these syllabuses to local needs or to the fact that the teachers may not be capable of putting them into practice or that the syllabuses and methods may not match the country's stage of educational development. (C. E. Beeby, *The Quality of Education in Developing Countries*.)

Element 9: MATERIALS CONSTRUCTION

This element is related both to element 8, SYLLABUS DESIGN and to element 7, PEDAGOGY, METHODOLOGY, INSTRUCTION, TEACHING. There is a case for treating this element separately, since it brings into consideration the great weight and influence of the educational publishing houses and radio and television, in addition to possessing inherent qualities of its own.

It is a practical requirement of the LL/LT process that learners should have available to them an extensive range of different materials. And it follows from the nature of teaching that the teacher should be able to choose this material from among an even greater range. The only practical way in which this can be brought about is by the existence of a massive industry of materials publishing, which in most countries relies on commercial firms. This is a difficult problem in countries whose educational budget is very small, and some such countries exercise various forms of restriction upon the availability of published materials from abroad. It is probably true, however, that there is a positive relation in any given country between effectiveness of teaching and the quantity of materials available to choose among. The bigger the choice, the more effective the teaching.

However that may be, all teaching materials need to possess certain characteristics—and these apply equally whether we are considering printed course-books, ancillary readers, visuals of many kinds, recordings, films, or any other kind of instructional materials. They need to be:

(i) *realistic* i.e. capable of being used by the teachers and learners; capable of being learned from; cheap enough to be available; actually in hand, not empty entries in an official list which never reach the learners;

(ii) *relevant* to the particular point in the learner's progress; to his aims and age-group;

(iii) *interesting* i.e. varied; on topics of interest to the learner; intellectually satisfying;

(iv) *encouraging* i.e. having the quality of making the learner feel he is making progress, or at least enjoying his learning;

(v) *compatible* with the approach being followed; with the teacher's attitudes.

We should point out that between them these last five elements embrace *the teacher*, as well as the teacher's professional activity. In the next element we shall see that the teacher whose professional skill falls below certain minimum standards becomes an impediment to the learner's progress. But that, we must assume, is the exception rather than the rule—or at least it is a condition which can be identified and presumably remedied by a further course of teacher training. Consequently we assume that 'the teacher' pervades the whole set of elements concerned with teaching: TEACHER TRAINING, APPROACH, PEDAGOGY, etc., SYLLABUS DESIGN, MATERIALS CONSTRUCTION. He or she does so either as an individual in personal contact with the learner (typically but not necessarily with a class of learners), or else at one remove from personal contact, as the designer of teaching materials, techniques, courses, etc.

All the five preceding elements can be regarded as jointly constituting the way in which the motive power of the public will, implemented through finance and organization, informed by the relevant professional disciplines, and channelled into the appropriate LL/LT type, is transformed into a prolonged and closely-directed effort of teaching and learning. Next we look at factors which may promote or reduce the effectiveness of this teaching/learning effort.

Element 10: CONSTRAINTS ON LL/LT ACHIEVEMENT

Suppose that in a given country all the elements so far considered were to have a high value: a particular language (let us say, English, for the sake of an example) is felt by the public to be of such value that all secondary school pupils should learn it (element 1); in the national education system, money is allocated for training teachers of English, paying their salaries, etc. (element 2); modern ideas on teaching English are available to the profession, for example through university and college staff (element 3); the appropriate LL/LT types are identified (element 4); teacher-training courses are provided which conform to international standards (element 5); a suitable approach is encouraged (element 6); good standards of teaching skill are available (element 7); realistic and relevant syllabuses are designed (element 8); and a wide range of suitable materials is available in schools and colleges (element 9). There remain a number of factors which may either act as constraints upon the effectiveness of the teacher/learning effort, or be capable of manipulation so as to increase that effectiveness. These constraints on achievement are the following:

(i) *total quantity of instruction*
(ii) *intensity of instruction*
(iii) *various impediments to learning and teaching*
(iv) *quality of the teacher*

Each of these merits a brief explanation.

(i) *Total quantity of instruction.* Since it is clear that language learning is not instantaneous, it must require time: there must be a minimum time for learning at a given rate to bring about a given level of attainment. Obviously, enough teaching/learning time must be provided for any particular criterion to be reached. Less obviously, it seems also to be the case that not too much time should be devoted to reaching a given criterion. A useful concept here (although unfortunately it seems to be as yet an abstract notion, incapable of being realized in quantifiable, observable terms) is what J. C. Catford has called the *mathon* (abbreviated *ma*) or 'unit of learning'. (Although Professor Catford has used this concept in his teaching over many years, I do not believe it has figured in his published work.) Suppose that to reach a given criterion of language learning requires 1000 *ma*; it might be determined that for a particular LL/LT type (see element 3) 1000 *ma* can be optimally taught and learned in 100 class hours. (Secondary observations might suggest that e.g. 5% of learners achieve the same criterion after only 70 hours, while 5% achieve only 70% of the criterion in the full 100 hours. Measurements of this kind are not in fact possible, but they would be extremely valuable.) So as a result of observation and experience, our 1000 *ma* are organized in 100 class hours, let us say at 3 hours per week for 33 weeks of a school year. But now suppose that in a particular school it is felt that this gives the learner too heavy a load, and instead the same criterion entailing 1000 *ma* is spread over two years, or 200 hours. There are indications that this decision might be followed by a drop in performance by the end of the course, on the grounds that 1000 *ma* are a quantity *too small* for 200 hours to support and therefore boredom will creep in, with the anti-learning consequences that all teachers recognize.

Many educators believe that this is already the case in the language teaching of many countries, and that better results on the present syllabus could be obtained by *reducing* the number of hours of instruction. Certainly it seems to be a common observation of school language courses that extension beyond about 3 or 4 years of overall duration is not usually accompanied by proportionate increases in terminal achievement.

This is an area where little is known with certainty but where a body of professional belief is growing which can be expressed thus: 'Every year of school language teaching beyond three years tends progressively to reduce the learner's eventual achievement, not to improve it.' No doubt this proposition, jestingly referred to as Strevens' Law, is an exaggeration and over-simplification. Nevertheless many people believe that a time/achievement relationship exists which ceases to be linear after a certain point and may change from positive (i.e. improvement) to negative (i.e. decline).

(ii) *Intensity of instruction.* A given total quantity of instruction can be concentrated into a short overall duration, or spread thinly over a long period. Do we know what effect differences of intensity bring about in the learning that takes place? There is little hard experimental evidence, but the growing consensus of those teachers who have experience of both higher- and lower-intensity teaching is that, within broad limits, as intensity goes up the learning-effectiveness of each hour of teaching goes up *more than proportionately*. In other words, at 25 hours per week, a 100-hour course engenders more learning than does the same course given at 5 hours per week. One can go further: it is possible that there is a lower limit below which the rate of learning per hour of teaching falls off disastrously. I would put this limit at about 4–5 hours per week. Below this rate of intensity it seems that the effectiveness of learning is much less, per hour, than above it. Perhaps there are too many opportunities for forgetting; or the learning does not reach a necessary minimum impetus or drive. Whatever the reason, 'thin' courses are notoriously ineffective. At the upper end of the intensity scale, more than approximately 18–20 hours per week requires special precautions to be taken against fatigue on the part of both learner and teacher. Higher rates of intensity are entirely possible and are often reported to be extremely effective, but they place special responsibilities on the teacher for ensuring that the quality of the teaching does not deteriorate, and in particular that the learner's stamina and continuing attention are closely watched and carefully nurtured. The important point for our present discussion is that intensity, like quantity, has a potential effect in raising or reducing the effectiveness of the learning/teaching process.

(iii) *Various impediments to teaching.* A number of physical and psychological factors can interfere quite drastically with learning and teaching. Some of these are obvious: *overcrowding*, for example. A class size of 100 is a prescription for very low average class rates of achievement; while a class size of 1 is a prescription for probable high rates of achievement. *Noise* is another factor of this kind. Heavy traffic noise is more pervasively damaging to the teaching of language, which for much of the time is carried by sound, than to some other subjects. In some parts of the world the sound of rain drumming on corrugated iron roofs is so overpowering that language learning stops, in practice if not in principle, for the duration of the monsoon season. *Distraction* is another factor. So is *fatigue*: for example, the class which is regularly timetabled for late on Friday afternoon can be largely written-off as a learning event. One of the most difficult impediments is *examination-neurosis*. Some learners (at all ages) become so anxious about their anticipated performance in exams that their learning is affected. This anxiety may originate either with the learner himself, or with his family, or even, unfortunately, with the teacher. All these impediments, and others which could be added to the list, diminish the learning that takes place. Conversely, removing them may have great effect in improving the achievement of the learners.

(iv) *The quality of the teacher.* In an earlier part of the discussion (on element 5) we considered TEACHER TRAINING and noticed that there exists a fairly general agreement about what constitutes an 'ideal' teacher. Here, in element 10, CONSTRAINTS, we encounter reality: how closely does the actual teacher in a given situation approach the ideal? It is one thing to train a man or woman to a high standard of professional ability: it is another to ensure that he or she maintains that standard, let alone that they improve on it, in the years that follow. Teaching can be, for some people, a difficult and trying profession, ill-paid, poorly-regarded in the community, frustrating, worrying. The teacher who views his job in this light is quite likely to deteriorate over the years in the standards he brings to the service of his pupils. A poor teacher is an impediment to the learning process—but what constitutes a poor teacher? There are perhaps three minimum requirements of a teacher which can be formulated, without which the teacher must be regarded as reducing the learner's chances of achieving his maximum rate of learning: (a) the teacher must display a 'non-discouraging' personality.

The test of this is pragmatic: if his pupils are in fact discouraged by him, the point is clear. (b) He must have an adequate command of the language he is teaching. Again the test is pragmatic: if he lacks command of the language in the form he needs for classroom use, if he suffers from hesitations and uncertainties in his control of the language that are recognized as such by his learners, if he makes errors or is inconsistent in his control of grammar, meaning or usage, then his grasp of the language is inadequate for his job and it becomes an impediment to the learning of his pupils. (c) He must display at least minimum skill as a teacher. Again, the question is answered by the teacher's actual performance. Do his pupils learn? If so, are they learning because of the teacher, irrespective of the teacher, or in spite of the teacher? In the last case the teacher is an impediment to the learning process. When it is this fourth impediment (i.e. poor quality of teacher) which is identified as occurring, one immediate remedy lies in renewed teacher training, and indeed one function of element 2 ADMINISTRATION AND ORGANIZATION, and element 5 TEACHER TRAINING is to provide prophylaxis against the occurrence of this impediment by making in-service re-training courses for teachers a normal expectation of the teacher's career.

It will be clear to the reader that this model of the language learning/teaching process regards both the *teacher* and the *learner* as contributing to the process, and as potentially either improving or diminishing its effectiveness according to the precise circumstances in each case. In the context of element 10, CONSTRAINTS ON LL/LT ACHIEVEMENT, the intention is to emphasize the fact that a teacher of inadequate quality may indeed diminish the learner's progress. But equally, a teacher of exceptionally good quality may improve the learner's progress and compensate for deficiencies elsewhere in the total system.

More generally, a given average level of competence among the whole population of teachers has consequences for the standards of teaching materials that are required. The very best teachers rely rather little upon materials prepared by other people, often making their own improvements or replacements and using the prescribed textbooks only as a general guide. The poorest teachers, on the other hand, rely totally on the teaching materials and are only as effective as the textbooks permit them to be. It is not unknown for textbooks to be written partly to help the teacher to improve the learner's progress, but also partly to serve as a form of in-service teacher training.

Interdependence exists between all the elements of our theoretical model, but nowhere is it more critical than between the quality of the teacher (part of element 10) and the nature of the teaching materials used (element 9).

Element 11: *THE LEARNER*

This is the point where the entire LL/LT process concentrates and has its effect. When a teacher teaches, it is with the aim and expectation that a learner learns. The learner is thus the focus and the end-point of all the elements 1 to 10 that have been considered in this chapter. But the learner is a human being, and not surprisingly he displays in this respect as in every other a number of differences between himself and other human beings. There is a tendency, in the wake of modern psycholinguistic studies of the way a small child learns his mother tongue, to act as if all language-learning human beings were just a set of identical, walking, talking language acquisition devices. Of course they all possess the wonderful human creativity that allows them to learn a language at all, but they also possess idiosyncrasies and distinctions that mark off one from another, as every teacher soon discovers. Leaving aside the range of psychological factors which a mental and emotional analysis would require, we need to distinguish (i) a common *potentiality* for language learning, and (ii) *personal variables*.

It seems to be inescapable that every normal human being has the *potentiality* to learn a foreign language (at least to achieve practical command of the spoken form). Whether the internal mechanism by which he does this is exactly the same as the mechanism by which he acquired his mother tongue is unimportant for the present discussion: what matters is that the potentiality exists. People can persuade themselves or be persuaded by others that they are incapable of learning a foreign language, but that does not alter the facts as they appear to be, namely that foreign language learning potentially exists in all human beings, at all ages.

The debate between those who argue that the infant's inherent 'language acquisition device' (LAD) remains with him unchanged throughout his life, and those who argue that the LAD atrophies during late childhood and therefore some other mental mechanism has to be used or developed in order to learn a foreign language, has always seemed to me an unrealistic dialectic. It is intuitively likely that the human individual's capacity for learning a language would alter in the course of his maturation in roughly the same ways that his other abilities alter. In that case, one would expect the child's LAD to partly endure and partly change: the language-learning mechanism of the older child would thus be partly *like* that of the infant and partly *different*—and this is what teachers observe. The polarity *changeless* versus *atrophying* seems an inadequate basis for discussion.

At the same time, and however much the teacher may wish to persuade himself that the learner learns *only* because the teacher teaches, we must also accept that people learn languages at least partly by themselves. If they are learning by 'picking the language up', then the unguided operation of the LAD is the sole source: most people under these conditions can acquire some degree of competence in the foreign language, but for the majority of them the procedure is slow in operation and patchy in quality. If they are learning from a teacher there are moments when they shut the teacher out (from lethargy, or boredom, or frustration, or even because they recognize a moment when the spontaneous operation of their own LAD may offer a quicker route to a specific piece of understanding) and give rein to their internal language acquisition mechanism. If he is using a 'self-study' method, he is confronted with an interesting mixture of techniques, in which his LAD is being manipulated, so to say, by a teacher who is disguised as the learner himself reading—vocally or silently—from a book.

The learner's potentiality for language learning, then, may be driven either solely by such experience of the language as the learner may encounter (e.g. as when picking up a language during a stay abroad) or solely as the result of the professionally-directed efforts of a teacher, or more often by a varying mixture of the two.

As to the personal variables which different people display, these are discussed in detail in Chapter 4. For the moment we shall limit ourselves to observing that learners differ greatly from one another in respect of their willingness to learn, their possession of any special abilities or defects, their previous experience of languages, and above all (from the point of view of the teacher) the 'manageability' of their learning.

Returning to our theoretical model, element 11, THE LEARNER, which is the focus of the immensely complex activity which is the LL/LT process, must assume that all learners have the potentiality to learn a language, but that there will certainly exist variations as between one learner and another and from time to time in the learning career of any individual. It is an essential part of the teacher's task to be aware of this and to have the professional knowledge and skill to enable him to help the individual learner at any given point of time, to maximize his rate of learning.

Element 12: EVALUATION

We have categorized language learning/teaching as a *process* in which something (i.e. the learner's command of the language) is being changed. Like most complex processes, LL/LT needs and possesses feedback systems which assess the progress of the change and supply information to those who are controlling the process (the teacher, or the learner himself if he is engaged in self-study learning) about how the learning is coming along, so that changes in the teaching can be made for the purpose of improving the learning. However, tests and examinations (and especially examinations, which unlike tests do not normally consist of objective measuring instruments) have come to fulfil a function different from that of a normal, regulatory feedback system. Instead of simply providing information about the learner's progress for the purpose of adjusting the teaching and so improving the learning, examinations are frequently used for purposes of social administration, selection for or against further education, certification of mere time served as a learner, provision of a ticket of admission to a range of jobs— in short, categorizing the individual against innumerable future events. This change of function can have damaging consequences for the success of language learning and teaching.

In the British tradition, at least, examinations have been allowed in many cases to dominate and distort the teaching, to the extent that teaching has often been centred on the syllabus for the exam rather than the syllabus for the teaching course. Perhaps surprisingly, these two syllabuses have rarely been the same. In many countries, especially in former British territories, the effective criterion for success in an English-language course has been to achieve the pass mark in an examination set and marked in Britain, with little or no account taken of the particular language syllabus followed in the schools overseas; sometimes the examination has been initially devised for British, native English-speaking candidates, and exported for use by foreign learners. Whatever the reasons for this (and they were often the highest educational motives) the result has been that many courses became 'exam-cramming', and the idea of a balanced language-learning syllabus was lost sight of. Fortunately, the current trend is towards the establishment of regional and local examination boards, and the reform of examination syllabuses in the hope of bringing about an improvement in the teaching. From the point of view of our theoretical study, we need to realize that evaluation takes many forms, some of them directly serving the teacher's needs for feedback information, some of them serving social and administrative needs, and some of them having unwanted and injurious effects upon teaching and learning.

We have now completed a survey, in simple outline, of the twelve principal elements that form the basis of this theoretical model. Of course, other models are conceivable, and models may be constructed from other standpoints. But the model described in this chapter is offered in the hope that it will encourage teachers and others to engage in theoretical studies of their profession. The elements and their inter-relationships are summarized in Diagram 1.

DIAGRAM I

A model of the LL/LT Process

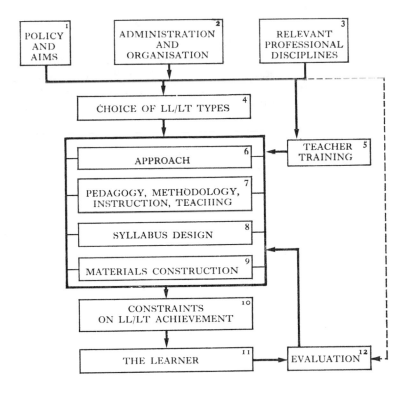

Acknowledgements

The original study forming the basis of this chapter was written during a period spent in 1974 as a Consultant in the Culture Learning Institute of the East-West Center, Honolulu, Hawaii. I am grateful to the Director and staff of the CLI for providing the conditions under which this and other papers could be written.

I am particularly grateful to the following for the assistance they gave me, sometimes unwittingly, in developing the ideas in this chapter: Dr H. H. Stern, Mr Richard Allwright, Mr Ronald Mackin, Mr Simon Murison-Bowie, Mr Larry Smith; also the M.A. and Ph.D. students in applied linguistics in the University of Essex, 1970–1973, especially Mr Kingsley Ervin, Dr Tony Shaw and Dr John Munby; students on the University of Cairo Linguistics Institute, 1973; and students in the Culture Learning Institute course for advanced teacher trainers, East-West Center, University of Hawaii, 1974. I am grateful also to Miss Patricia Kim for typing the original script and to my wife for preparing the diagram.

3 On defining applied linguistics

Inter-disciplinary studies, however well-merited their existence, often have one awkward characteristic: it is not easy to find a suitable name for them. The neighbourhood of linguistics has been particularly fertile ground for such developments and at least three important new fields have emerged and become fully established: *psycholinguistics, sociolinguistics, applied linguistics*. The first two names are reasonably self-explanatory, since *psycho-* clearly suggests links with psychology and *socio-* with social theory. The term *applied linguistics*, by contrast, is potentially either obscure or misleading, since (a) more than simply the application of theory is involved, and (b) other disciplines than linguistics are centrally concerned.

Not that being self-evident is always essential in a name, as long as it is seen to be a *label* rather than a technical term to be taken literally, *au pied de la lettre*. The label *language laboratory* is in a somewhat similar case, since it is less a laboratory, in any literal interpretation, than simply a specially-equipped classroom. Similarly, the meaning of applied linguistics is not to be arrived at by the simple conjunction of the meanings of the words of which it is composed.

What defines applied linguistics is the range of intellectual and practical activities with which it is concerned, and these are nowhere more authoritatively displayed than in the programmes and proceedings of the international congresses held under the auspices of AILA (l'Association Internationale de Linguistique Appliquée) in Nancy (1964), Cambridge (1969), Copenhagen (1971) and Stuttgart (1975). But it is a poor answer to the question 'What *is* applied linguistics?' to refer the enquirer to volumes of conference proceedings.

Fundamental definitions in any science often end in apparent circularity, as when Professor Daniel Jones enquired of his zoologist colleagues how they would define *a dog* and received the reply 'A four-footed mammal recognized as a dog by another dog'. This chapter attempts a definition with no pretence at being fundamental but based on an analysis of the intellectual and practical bases employed by applied linguists in their professional work. The definition is framed as a set of five propositions.

1. *Applied linguistics has a basis in theory and principle*

It is not simply a body of techniques, procedures, practicalities; although none of these are shunned by applied linguistics, it is an essential characteristic of the profession that its members seek the underlying principles, rationales, generalizations, hypotheses, theories, which account for and help to explain the vast diversity of practical activities with which they are confronted.

2. *These bases are multiple*

Applied linguistics seeks and accepts illumination from any and every source: it is essentially multi-disciplinary, as indeed it is forced to be by the varied nature of its preoccupations. At various times and in relation to various tasks, applied linguistics looks to linguistics, psychology, neuro-physiology, information theory, social theory (especially sociology and anthropology), education, philosophy, logic and scientific method. It is not *the whole of* each of these disciplines that is involved, simply the relevant areas of the appropriate discipline or group of disciplines. Consequently no single discipline monopolizes the theory and methodology of applied linguistics, not even theoretical linguistics, though if there is any single discipline more frequently relevant than the others (and most obviously appropriate as 'core training' for the aspiring applied linguist) it is linguistics—yet even here a broad approach to linguistics is of greater value than awareness of but a single school of thought. It is this multiple basis of interlocking disciplines which makes applied linguistics—and *only* applied linguistics—capable of responding in a principled way to *any* language-related problem.

3. *Applied linguistics is not restricted to an interest in the learning and teaching of languages*

It is undoubtedly true that the largest single area of concern and the largest source of financial backing lies in the study of language learning and teaching, but it is essential to be aware that applied linguistics is in principle interested in and competent to approach *any* language-related problem. Thus, speech pathology, translation (including automatic translation), the design of writing systems, national language planning policy, various facets of communication research, and many other problems, fall within the area of interest of applied linguistics. It is in fact a positive gain to the language teaching aspect of applied linguistics that the learning and teaching of languages is far from being the sole focus of concern. Nevertheless it is this language teaching aspect which provides the greatest single body of support and the biggest set of practical tasks for applied linguistics.

4. Applied linguistics re-defines itself afresh for each task

Because it has numerous aims and multiple bases, applied linguistics can hardly have a single, unchanging nature. Rather to the contrary: the precise aims of a particular task determine which of the theoretical bases are likely to be the most relevant and in which proportions, and this in turn will affect the methodology and approach of the applied linguist.

In relation to the learning and teaching of languages, applied linguistics defines itself as having three main components:

> (i) *the underlying disciplines;*
> (ii) *teaching techniques;*
> (iii) *aids and equipment.*

(i) *The underlying disciplines.* The most relevant disciplines are probably those of *linguistics* (especially *descriptive linguistics* and *socio-* and *psycholinguistics*), some branches of *psychology,* and *education,* including the socio-economic study of education in relation to stages of national development.

(ii) *Teaching techniques.* The disciplines by themselves meet only part of the applied linguist's needs. It is necessary that he should also be familiar with the full range of existing approaches, methods and techniques of teaching languages, as well as with new developments, trends, experiments; and that he should be able to bring theory and practice into meaningful relationship.

(iii) *Aids and equipment.* The third element comprises the artefacts which the teacher can use in his search for ways to improve learning and aid teaching. This knowledge includes not simply being competent in the practical operation of gramophone, tape recorder, language lab, radio, videotape, etc., but also having a sufficient understanding of their design principles and of their limitations as well as their advantages, and being aware of their place in the total scheme of learning and teaching languages.

Applied linguistics in relation to language teaching, then, provides a combination and blend of the most valuable elements in theory, method and equipment. And these elements have been elaborated and refined, over the past fifteen years, in a way that provides a sophisticated answer to the perennial problem, 'What is the relation between linguistics and language teaching?' (See especially J. P. B. Allen and S. Pit Corder, *The Edinburgh Course in Applied Linguistics,* 4 vols.) This is the 'ready-made package' of professional assistance referred to in discussing element 3 of the theoretical model of the language learning/teaching process, in Chapter 2.

5. *Applied linguistics is dynamic, not static*

This flexible, open-ended definition of applied linguistics has two principal advantages: first, it permits maximum adaptability to the precise needs of each different task; and second, it ensures that applied linguistics remains dynamic, changing by the addition of new sources of illumination or by incorporating new developments within existing components.

Applied linguistics is at present the only discipline which fulfils this multi-based, inter-disciplinary, language-related function. It can be justifiably proud of the success it has achieved so far, and applied linguists can ensure continuance of this success by keeping an open, informed, professional outlook upon their theoretical bases.

4 Language acquisition, language learning, language teaching

This chapter is concerned with the relevance to language teaching of recent psycholinguistic research into the way in which the infant acquires its mother tongue. In particular there have emerged a set of related ideas which language teachers cannot ignore. Briefly stated, they are as follows:

(i) it is a universal characteristic of the human species that its members acquire command of a language, unless they suffer from an abnormality or impediment;

(ii) the acquisition of a language for the first time occurs during the age-range of around $1\frac{1}{2}$–6 years, never earlier and only in exceptional cases beginning any later;

(iii) the onset of language is linked chronologically with the later stages of anatomical development of the brain;

(iv) it seems that an individual child who has not acquired any language by the age of puberty will not adequately do so thereafter—that there may be a 'critical age' for first language acquisition;

(v) the child's command of its mother tongue progresses by stages from its first meaningful sounds towards an 'adult-like' command of the language, albeit over a restricted range of the language compared with that of the adult;

(vi) language acquisition occurs without the aid of formal or institutionalized instruction;

(vii) children acquiring a given first language do so with remarkable similarity between one another in the stages and sequences of their language development, and in the ages at which they achieve control of particular features of language;

(viii) a comparison of language acquisition across different languages shows considerable similarity in sequences of development, irrespective of which particular language is being acquired— there is a degree of 'universality' in patterns of acquisition;

(ix) it is possible to regard a child's progress through the period of his acquisition of his mother tongue as consisting of a series of

successively closer approximations towards adult command of
the language, a series of stages of 'interlanguage', or of 'pro-
visional grammars' of the language;

(x) under these circumstances a small child's deviations from the
adult's norm in the language are to be regarded not as errors
but as 'milestones along the road of progress'.

There are of course many other strands to the sophisticated programmes of research in psycholinguistics, but the foregoing selection
of points embodies most of the ideas of obvious—or apparent—
relevance to the language teacher. In order to decide on the importance
of these ideas for his work, and the changes, if any, which he should
make in his outlook and activity, the language teacher needs to know,
first, whether the child's language acquisition process continues unchanged after the 'critical age' for first language acquisition; second,
whether the process remains unchanged for additional, subsequent
languages; and third, whether the process occurring during first
language acquisition, in informal conditions, is the same as that which
takes place in formal, institutionalized instruction.

In the wake of this research there has been a tendency to regard
'second language acquisition'—learning foreign languages—as an extension and continuation of mother tongue acquisition, and even to
doubt whether the teacher of foreign languages has any function other
than keeping the learner awake, given that the individual possesses a
'language acquisition device'.

It seems to me that this point of view ignores a distinction between
two crucially different types of language acquisition: between on the
one hand those who 'pick up' a foreign language during prolonged contact with people using it, and on the other hand those who learn a
foreign language within a framework of deliberate and organized
instruction. In the first case there is every reason to expect that the
mechanism of language acquisition is indeed broadly similar to that of
the infant, subject to variations as a result of greater maturity. Many
millions of people alive today have picked up a greater or lesser command of one or more foreign languages in this way. But many millions
more have learned a greater or lesser command of one or more foreign
languages in the circumstances of the second case, i.e. in conditions of
deliberate instruction, which are different in many respects from those
of first language acquisition.

In this chapter, then, we shall consider the nature of the foreign
language learning/teaching process in its institutionalized form, in
contrast with first language acquisition; we shall propose that the
differences are so many and so fundamental that the term *acquisition*
should be used only to refer to untutored first language acquisition by
the young child and to equivalent processes such as 'picking up a

language' at a later age without the involvement of a teacher; and that *learning* and *teaching* should be used for the institutionalized process.

The language learning/language teaching process is a complex with three principal determinants:

    (i) the learner;
    (ii) the teacher;
    (iii) the situation in which they interact.

FACTORS CONTRIBUTED BY THE LEARNER

These are of two main kinds:

(a) those which relate to the learner's identity and which the teacher can do little or nothing about, at least from one moment to the next—these we shall call the learner's *static qualities*;

(b) those which relate to the 'manageability of his learning' in the sense that they offer information to the teacher on the basis of which he may choose one teaching technique rather than another—these features we shall call the learner's *dynamic qualities*.

The Learner's Static Qualities

1. *Potentiality for learning languages*

It seems to be a reasonable hypothesis that every learner without exception up to the onset of senility who can acquire his mother tongue is potentially capable of learning a foreign language—i.e. of achieving a reasonable command of the spoken language. The dimension of age results in a difference of learning style but does not fundamentally impair the quality of potentiality for learning languages. This hypothesis of universal potentiality agrees in broad terms with the equivalent psycholinguistic hypothesis of first language acquisition, while standing outside any detailed discussion about how much of the acquisition mechanism is innate—i.e. is present at birth.

2. *Age*

Age—maturational age rather than chronological age—is an important variable, especially in respect of the physiological development of the brain, of emotional development, and of social experience. All these, taken together with the increased total experience of language that accompanies age, affect the learning of a foreign language.

3. *Willingness to give the necessary effort*

This is a complex group of qualities some of which may be inherent, others of which can be improved by the teacher's pains or by external influence.

4. *Learning stamina (i.e. the ability to maintain the learning effort for a period of time)*
This is a quality of the learner which varies not only between individuals but also at different stages in the development of a single individual. Younger learners in general have less stamina (as evidenced by a shorter attention-span, for example) than older learners.

5. *Special abilities or defects*
There exists a range of qualities of temperament, preference and interest which affect the individual's profile as a learner. Differences of *memory*, of *preference for eye over ear* or vice versa, of *'verbal ability'*, of possession of what is often called *'a good ear'*, of *ability to mimic*, of *competence in guessing*, even major differences of *intelligence*—all these seem to affect the learner's progress and achievement. Defects of *hearing* or *sight* can also be important.

6. *Previous linguistic experience:* (a) *in the mother tongue*
The extent of the learner's command of his primary language, including the question of whether he has learned to read and write in it, and his experience and awareness of diversity such as accents, dialects, scales of formality-informality, etc., will affect his progress in the foreign language. So also will the extent of cognateness or similarity between his primary language and the foreign language and between his own culture and the foreign culture.
(b) *Previous experience of foreign languages*
There is fair agreement, though it is based solely on anecdotal evidence, that each additional foreign language learned presents a lighter learning load than the previous one. It is certainly the case that previous experience of one or more foreign languages affects to some extent the learning of another, and the nature of this influence depends in part on the relationship and similarities of the languages concerned.

7. *Experience of learning in general*
Similarly, the individual's experience of learning in general, and of 'learning to learn', have a considerable though unmeasurable effect on his progress in a foreign language.

The Learner's Dynamic Qualities

These are the variables which help the teacher to make decisions about the best way of managing the individual's learning.

1. *Personal learning rate*

It has long been customary for teachers to refer to 'fast learners' and 'slow learners'. In fact there are many possibilities between these extremes; furthermore, not only do individuals differ, but one individual may change his rate of learning from one stage in his learning career to another. (Learning rate is tied in with stamina: it is possible to encourage a learner to learn at his personal maximum rate, but at this rate his stamina is likely to be reduced.) The teacher seeks to promote the optimum rate for each individual, that is, the highest rate of learning that does not impair his stamina.

2. *Preferred learning styles* (*or 'strategies'*)

Individuals have different preferences for the kind of learning activity which they can engage in at their optimum rate. Some like rote-learning, some dislike it; some enjoy problem solving; some prefer discovery procedures; some learn best if they are extending the coverage of the rules they can already operate; most prefer interest and variety in the learning task. Teachers can become familiar with the preferred learning styles of their pupils and can optimize learning accordingly.

3. *Minimum success-need*

There are great differences in the extent and frequency with which learners require to be encouraged or reassured or consoled by evidence of success, and this quality is often related to learning rate: insufficient evidence of success is usually followed by a drop in the rate of learning as well as by diminished confidence and interest.

4. *Self-view as a language learner*

Learners vary greatly in their attitudes towards themselves as learners and in their expectations of achievement. These attitudes are produced partly by their own previous experience, partly by the comments of friends and family, partly by the comments of the teacher and fellow-learners. When his self-view is optimistic or pessimistic to an unrealistic extent it can become an impediment to the learner's progress.

5. *Relations with teachers*

The progress of many learners is very sensitive to their relationships with teachers. Some learn equally well (or badly) no matter who the teacher is; some reach their optimum learning rate more readily with some teachers than with others; some find difficulty in relating to *any* teachers. And the degree of effect which the relationships have upon learning may itself change from one period of time to another: for example, adolescents are especially liable to strong emotional feelings towards or against particular teachers, and these feelings at that age have an inordinate effect upon the learner's achievement.

FACTORS CONTRIBUTED BY THE TEACHER

These are of two types:

(i) factors arising from the nature of the task of language teaching;
(ii) factors arising from the teacher's individuality.

There are implications here, which we should be aware of, for the argument of this chapter. Having contrasted those learners who 'pick up' a language with those who learn a language in conditions of organized instruction, we then suggested that the second group, but not the first, are affected in their language learning process by three sets of factors: factors contributed by the learner; factors contributed by the teacher; and factors contributed by the circumstances in which learner and teacher come together. Now we are saying that among the factors contributed by the teacher are a set whose basis lies in the nature of the task of language teaching. To summarize 'the task of language teaching' is to presuppose that beneath the vast diversity of languages, aims, methods, etc., there exists a common, world-wide acceptance of what the educational task is.

And there is a further implication that the commonly agreed task of language teaching produces conditions and constraints upon the teacher which are themselves a part of the essential differences between the *acquisition* of languages and the *learning* of languages, as we have distinguished them.

How, then, can we define the task of language teaching? Here is a working summary, followed by brief comments on some of its elements:

The task of language teaching is, typically, to manage the learning of an individual (or more often, successive groups of individuals) within an institutional framework so that they can achieve in a given time-span a best approximation to a defined sub-set of the total abilities of a native speaker of the foreign language. The crucial elements of this definition are these:

(a) *typically:* there are of course occasional variations from this type, but when people refer to 'language teaching' it is this typical set of elements they refer to;

(b) *to manage learning:* not just teaching, and not just permitting learning, but by deliberate, knowledgeable activity promoting and managing the learning process;

(c) *individuals or groups of individuals:* the language learner is an individual, but the teacher typically has to deal with a whole class;

(d) *an institutional framework:* teachers do not spring fully-trained out of the earth but are trained, constrained, paid, pensioned, encouraged and restricted by a massive framework of organization which permits the achievement of success but also the possibility of failure;

(e) *a given time-span:* language learning and teaching takes place within an arbitrary time-scale, often too short for best results, but sometimes perhaps too long.

(f) *an approximation to . . . a native speaker:* the aim of achieving native-speaker ability in the foreign language is usually a myth, a platonic ideal at best, replaced in practice by a tacitly agreed lesser target (usually and inadequately defined by an examination) for each different stage of learning;

(g) *a defined sub-set:* learning rarely attempts to embrace 'the whole of' a language nor to achieve the full range of mastery of his language which a native speaker can command, and the teaching syllabus is in practice a definition of a particular sub-set of the language in place of the total abilities of the native speaker. The teaching and learning of literature, or translation, or English for specific purposes, are some examples of 'defined sub-sets' of a language.

Factors Arising from the Teacher's Task

1. *Purpose*
The teacher knows and accepts the purpose of the learner's activity, whereas the learner himself very often does not. The consequences of this difference are frequently very important for the course of the learning and of the teaching.

2. *Time-scale*
The teacher is engaged in a time-compression task, by contrast with first language acquisition. In a total of 100 or 300 or 500 hours—rarely more—the teacher is helping the learner to achieve a command of the language roughly like that which the child acquires in his first language after, say, 6000 to 8000 hours of acquisition time.

3. *Expectations*
The teacher can provide the learner with expectations which are realistic, encouraging but not extravagant.

4. *Monitoring progress*
The teacher can assess progress, identify gaps and errors, vary the pace or the content or the kind of activity, etc., so as to manage the learning both of the individual learner and of the class as a whole.

Factors Arising from the Teacher's Individuality

It is necessary to assume that the normal case falls within the limits of what constitutes a 'good teacher', in the sense in which we used the term in Chapter 2, i.e. that he or she possesses a non-discouraging personality, has an adequate command of the language being taught, and can exercise adequate skills as a teacher. The good teacher, then, brings to the language learning/language teaching situation at least the following elements:

1. *The establishment of confidence, morale,* a set towards learning and being taught. This includes the maintenance of *interest* and *motivation*.
2. *The continual adjustment of teaching to fit the learner's needs,* both in terms of the point of attainment reached and also in terms of the learner's profile of individuality, so that he maintains progress at his optimum learning rate towards the maximum goal which he as a learner is capable of attaining.

THE LANGUAGE LEARNING/LANGUAGE TEACHING SITUATION

The third major way in which language learning differs from language acquisition is in the situation within which it takes place. Here the factors which are at work relate

   (i) to the situation of the individual learner and
   (ii) to influences from the community at large.

The Situation of the Individual

These are presented as polarities.

1. *Institutional versus Familial*
Acquisition occurs in the framework of family life (or its substitute) whereas learning with a teacher occurs in a non-familial institution; the consequences of this difference, consequences which are psychological and social in nature, are considerable.

2. *Group Activity versus Solo Activity*
In particular, learning with a teacher removes the learner from his place in the family, where, during the age of language acquisition, he has frequently been the focus of attention and affection. It makes him instead a single member of a group of equals, within which his standing and role are established at least partly by his successful participation in peer-group activities.

3. *Time-constrained versus Time-free*
Language acquisition knows nothing of the clock. Language learning is timetabled, divided into timed segments, set overall within the time-compression framework mentioned earlier. Opportunities for language acquisiton occur as an unordered, continuous trickle; in language learning they present themselves as intermittent showers at pre-ordained times, sometimes with gaps of weeks or months without learning.

4. *Quotidian versus Occasional*
Babies do not take days off. Consequently acquisition is a pervasive and integral part of daily personal life, 365 days in the year; language learning takes place only occasionally, only within a set portion of waking hours, and unrelated to the ongoing flow of personal daily life.

5. *Vital versus Peripheral*
Acquisition takes place as part of understanding, taking part in, communicating about and being communicated with about daily personal life; language learning being unrelated to daily personal life, it is essentially peripheral. (I prefer these terms to 'natural' versus 'artificial', because although the classroom is clearly different from home life, it seems perverse to call 'artificial' a situation which is normal to the individual for some 1000 hours per year for up to fifteen or even twenty years.)

Influences from the Community at Large

These influences relate (a) to the learner, (b) to the teacher, (c) to the language being taught, and (d) to the organizational framework of learning and teaching.

(a) *Influences on the learner*
  (i) *Attitudes towards education* in general, towards foreign-language learning in particular, and also towards the individual as a learner of a specific language. ('Johnny is learning French/shouldn't be learning French/will succeed in learning French/won't succeed in learning French', etc.)
  (ii) *The consequences of social class.* Observations of the kind studied by Bernstein and others, about the differences of home language in different classes of society, have consequences for the individual as a language learner.

(b) *Influences on the teacher*
  (i) *The status of teachers.* This will affect the morale of the teacher, the general intellectual standards of those who make up the teaching profession, and the professional skill of teachers of languages.
  (ii) *The standards of teacher training.* These, too, reflect an influence from the community upon the teacher.

(c) *Influences relating to the language taught*
  (i) *The status of the foreign language.* A language with high status, or one which is taken for granted, will be learned and taught differently and with different rates of success from one which is disliked.
  (ii) *Extent of the language in the community.* Attitudes apart, the sheer quantity of exposure of the learner to the language he is learning has an effect on his progress.

(d) *The organizational framework of learning and teaching*
The paradox of administration. The community, through its educational authorities, can permit (or impose) conditions which make it difficult or impossible to learn, and difficult or impossible to teach. The child acquiring its first language stands largely outside this kind of community influence; organized language learning, on the other hand, can be promoted, or permitted, or actually prevented, according to the excellence of the administrative and organizational framework.

Conclusions

The foregoing summary of the special features of language learning and teaching is also a catalogue of differences (with the sole exception of the learner's potentiality for language) between the universe of discourse of psycholinguistics and the universe of discourse of language teaching.

The first conclusion drawn from the argument is that psycholinguistic research into child language acquisition, important though it undoubtedly is, concerns itself with a set of phenomena crucially different from those of learning a language with a teacher.

The second conclusion is that in order to avoid confusion the term *acquisition* is best restricted to 'picking up' a language, particularly in the case of the child's acquisition of his first language but sometimes also in relation to the older learner who picks up a language in an informal way; and that *learning* and *teaching* should be used to refer to the complementary aspects of institutionalized language learning.

The third conclusion is that the circumstances of language acquisition are different from those of language learning in so many aspects that there is no reason to suppose that language teaching need be directly affected by research on language acquisition. Some of the more important features of psycholinguistic research may indeed eventually be incorporated into language learning/language teaching procedures, but there is no dependency relation between language teaching and psycholinguistics which ordains this to occur. Language learning and teaching require their own theoretical treatment in terms of their own features and variables—and that, of course, is what they are at last receiving within the multi-disciplinary framework of applied linguistics.

Part Two

Methodology and Teacher Training

5 British and American methodology in English language teaching: similarities and differences

The two principal resource countries providing teachers, teacher trainers, techniques and theories for teaching English the world over are Britain and the United States. Of the other English-speaking countries, Australia, New Zealand and perhaps especially Canada are increasing their contribution, but for some time to come Britain and the U.S. will remain the chief source of manpower and of professional inspiration.

It is not until one works closely with professionals from the opposite side of the Atlantic that the nature and extent of similarities and differences between the two become evident. Then one discovers that although the U.S. and Britain share the same language, and although they broadly share a common outlook on education and teaching, their different experience in different areas of the world, their separate historical and intellectual strands of development, and their cultural differences, combine to produce a distinctive ELT profession in each country.

This chapter presents an outline of British views and practices in the field of English language teaching, and indicates some of the contrasts between them and their American counterparts. The summary is not, of course, an apology. On the contrary, the British ELT tradition has considerable virtues: its flexibility and dislike of dogma helps the teacher to avoid transient fashions and violent swings of approach; its *pedagogical professionalism* gives the teacher a profound and valuable conception of the teaching process and of the teacher's role; without claiming spectacular achievements, the British ELT tradition nevertheless has a long record of steady, reasonable success, above all in teaching pupils overseas up to age 17 or 18. It seems to many British ELT specialists that the American approach, with its virtues of greater *disciplinary professionalism* and its stricter methodology, has been especially successful in teaching young adults, within the U.S.A.

There is a danger of over-simplification here, because within the broad lines of the American profession of English language teaching there exists a group of institutions and individuals—at UCLA, Columbia

University Teachers' College, the East-West Center in Hawaii, the Ontario Institute for Studies in Education, to name some of the best-known examples—whose interest in teaching young children, in training teachers for that educational level, and in making links with school English programmes in countries overseas, give them affinities with what is done in Britain as much as with the North American tradition. Consequently any differences and contrasts suggested in this chapter between British and American practice must be thought of as being typical, but not universal.

First, we need to sort out our divergent terminologies. The American terms TEFL, TESL, TESOL, TESOLD have no precise counterparts in British usage. The principal British cover term is *English language teaching* (ELT), which normally excludes English as the mother tongue. Within ELT we make a distinction between *English as a foreign language* (EFL) and *English as a second language* (ESL), and this distinction reflects important differences in the ELT situation, and hence in the methods and techniques most commonly used. We shall return to this distinction shortly.

The professional affiliations of ELT have changed in the past twenty-five years. Originally, teachers of English overseas (because it was overseas, not in Britain, that the great majority of British ELT took place) felt themselves akin to teachers of English as the mother tongue, and especially to teachers of English literature. Most British teachers engaged overseas had a degree in English literature and few had any specialist training as teachers of English language. Nowadays there is a well-established ELT profession, both within Britain and overseas but dependent on British support; this profession includes high-level specialist training courses which treat English not as the mother tongue but as a subsequently acquired language. Thus the affiliations of ELT are now more with *foreign language teaching* (FLT) of which ELT is seen as a special case.

Within British ELT it is a basic assumption that the nature of learning and teaching in any given teaching situation is affected by a great number of variables, and that in consequence a different choice among a wide range of possible procedures and methods will turn out to be appropriate in different teaching/learning situations. The notion of a single 'best' method, one which would claim to be equally effective in all circumstances, has always been rejected by British (and European) ELT, partly for the theoretical reasons outlined in Chapter 1, partly on what seem intuitively to be obvious practical grounds (i.e. 'it doesn't work like that') and partly because on a more intellectual plane British and European thought generally takes a 'pluralist' view of the truth: students are encouraged not to seek the unique 'right' view of the truth, but rather to recognize that the truth exists in many guises and in many 'right' views. The student seeks aspects of the truth wherever he can find it and is sceptical of any view which claims to have a monopoly of the truth.

Aside from what may be a philosophical difference between American TEFL and British ELT and turning to our differing historical experiences, the British ELT profession has been concerned especially with training and supplying British teachers to overseas countries, and with giving training in Britain to teachers from overseas countries, both of the EFL and the ESL type. In addition, there is a long and powerful tradition of supporting teacher training colleges overseas by supplying and training expatriate and local staff. This has been especially the case in former British territories, most of which are or were ESL areas, and where in many cases the school syllabuses and coursebooks are either written by British authors or at least modelled on their tradition. There is also a sizeable and growing British effort in EFL countries, notably in Europe and the Middle East. American experience has more often been located inside the United States, teaching adult immigrants or foreign students; when the effort has been directed overseas it has generally been more in the foreign language than in the second language situation —though there are some major exceptions to this observation, e.g. in the Philippines and American Samoa.

Accepting that generalizations are inaccurate and may be unfair to individual cases on both sides of the Atlantic, the respective activities and their degree of similarity can be summarized in the following way: (i) the British and the Americans each possess a strong 'second language' component of overseas work with children and in teacher training, which is closely similar on both sides and includes many personal Anglo-American links; (ii) the 'foreign language' components, on the other hand, exhibit considerable differences, partly in that American TEFL has been principally concerned with teaching adults within the United States while British EFL has been more often engaged in teaching in schools and colleges in 'foreign language' countries, and partly in the principles and practices that each side projects. (Again, we must note a sizeable exception in the form of a growing 'private sector' of schools and colleges within Britain which cater for the needs of adult students from overseas. This is a parallel to American ELT, though in Britain, which is not an 'immigration' country, the numbers of students are far fewer than in America.)

One further geo-linguistic observation: British ELT activity has followed a path of continuous development, without major change, through from the 1920's, in the tradition of Sweet, Jespersen, Palmer, Hornby. American TEFL, too, often acknowledges roots in Sweet, Jespersen and Palmer, but it has additionally been through a period of massive change. During a period of domination by Bloomfieldian linguistics and Skinnerian psychology the attitudes of American teachers towards methodology became very different from the attitudes of their British colleagues, in several important respects. And during this same period there were carried out a number of important American projects for assisting overseas countries in establishing or modernizing the English language programmes followed in their school systems. Now that American TEFL opinion is moving away from its structuralist-behaviourist principles, two effects can be seen: first, the outlook of teachers on both sides of the Atlantic seems once again to be converging a good deal; but second, the structuralist-behaviourist syllabuses established in many countries during the audio-lingual era are being left high and dry, without—as it were—philosophical support. And this is happening just at the time when the syllabuses in many countries are coming up for revision and reform.

To return to the summary of British ELT, the bulk of what follows in this chapter relates to teachers of English as a *second* language, both teachers from Britain working in ESL areas and teachers from such areas who have been trained in the British tradition. The summary is largely true also of British teachers of English as a *foreign* language, with the reservation that EFL teachers are on the whole more strongly grounded in theory, and are perhaps also less free to be pedagogically inventive than their ESL colleagues.

This difference stems largely from the different circumstances of ESL and EFL teaching. When English is a *second* language, as we have seen, it generally has an important role in education (often it is the medium of instruction in some sectors of the school system) in the law courts, in business; the common-sense utility of learning English is obvious even to the boy or girl at school, so that motivation for achievement is higher; general public levels of fluency in English are higher; there is often a British-based educational system, and even more often the pupils work towards a British-based final examination; at the same time there are often local restricted varieties of English (pidgins, pp. 139–41, local dialects, frequently local accents) which pose special problems for the ESL teacher. But when English is a *foreign* language, it is no more important or prominent than other foreign languages; there is no obvious reason for learning it, so that motivation is low; there is little exposure to English outside the classroom; the teacher of English as one among several foreign languages exposes it to the pedagogical customs of the country concerned—as for example in Germany, where English is required to be taught 'for understanding the Anglo-Saxon mind'—and this dilutes the effectiveness of the British teaching traditions we are concerned with in this paper; only native-like performance is acceptable as the EFL target, and this often seems to the learner to be remote and difficult to achieve. Differences in outlook are inevitable as between ESL and EFL; the summary which follows is more closely aligned with the second language, though it is not vastly inaccurate for the foreign language situation.

A Summary of Current British ELT Practice

1. *Approach (i.e. commitment to positions of principle, theory, methodology)*

The approach is *pragmatic*, not *dogmatic*. The primary test of excellence is 'Does it work?' not 'Is it theoretically justifiable?' Teachers are of course aware of principles and theories: postgraduate courses in particular provide excellent teaching of theory. But teachers in Britain are by and large hostile to the view that practice is just the application of theory, and they regard most current theories in linguistics, psychology and psycholinguistics as being pedagogically naïve and therefore largely irrelevant. A theory of language teaching, on the other hand, with well-motivated links to specific areas of linguistics and psychology —*that* might be more attractive. In the meantime, British teachers retain a considerable scepticism about any single school of thought in theoretical linguistics and psychology being an adequate guide to language teaching, and many of them now make use of a mix of elements taken from e.g. structural linguistics, transformational theory, behaviourist and cognitive psychology, Chomskyan psycholinguistics, Hallidayan systemic and functional theory, Firthian ideas on varieties and on 'context of situation', sociolinguistics, and so on.

The teacher is believed to have a role in the management of learning, but again this role is not seen in relation to any particular established theory of linguistics or psychology. Many teachers, especially in ESL, regard themselves as educators, not simply as instructors; the teacher ideally has a function in the total intellectual and moral development of the learner, not just in his learning of a language.

2. *Aims (i.e. targets of achievement for the learner)*

These are increasingly tailored to what is realistically capable of being achieved, and to locally-agreed targets for the learner and his community. Newly-independent nations in the ESL condition (Zambia is an example) and other countries, too, are often willing to reconsider the terminal aims that are proper to their capabilities and needs. As a rule, aims are stated in terms of the so-called 'skills' of language: understanding, speaking, reading and writing. But many people now feel that these labels are too gross and that a more delicate analysis is needed, to show what the learner is to be able to *do* with his language: e.g. 'aural comprehension for rapid gathering of important facts in a face-to-face encounter', as a sub-division of *understanding*. All these 'skills' are likely to be specified for inclusion, but in differing proportions in different countries. In general, targets for writing tend to be lower, targets for reading tend to be valued more highly, than before.

In most ESL countries, the aims in practice are generally focused on public examinations, either actually administered from Britain or modelled on our example. For thirty years, the consuming importance to the learner of passing the exam (because if you don't pass in English you don't get a job, or go to college) has perverted the teaching of English. Now there are signs that countries and examiners realize that more enlightened examining brings about more enlightened teaching.

3. *English in the total curriculum*

English has normally been taught as a part of a broad general education, oriented towards the humanities. It used to be linked with, and often incorporated, an introduction to the study and appreciation of English literature, and this constituted the principal justification for teaching the language. However, over the past twenty-five years the strength of this justification has evaporated; nowadays a much stronger justification for learning English is provided by the evident usefulness of having a practical, communicative command of the language. In some areas as a result English literature has been largely or completely dropped from the curriculum, or has been replaced by 'literature *in* English', so as to bring into the educational area works such as those by African or Indian writers, and also literature translated into English.

A further change in the justification for teaching English is taking place in some localities: there is emerging the concept of teaching only such selections of English as are needed for vocational needs or other special purposes, e.g. for studying science, technology or business. The outstanding example of this trend is the Singapore Primary Integrated Materials Pilot Project, in which English is taught through and for science, at the beginning level. (See Chapters 8 and 9.)

There is also developing a feeling that henceforth the educated citizen needs to be multilingual, with English an obvious choice for one of his languages. So, from the opinion that the education of foreign children must include English literature, educators have swung to the opinion that the education of all children must include an international language, *for use*. The deliberate use of English for certain school subjects (as in Swaziland and Kenya) and the proliferation of multilingual schooling (e.g. the 'International' schools in Europe) are all examples of this. Among this change, literature retains a place, but henceforward it will be provided in greater depth, for fewer but more advanced, Arts-oriented students.

4. *Speech/writing*

English is taught in both spoken and written form. Oral-only syllabuses are not found except for a few specialized purposes. The teaching of speech runs ahead of teaching the written equivalent by a variable amount in the early stages. Thereafter it is not dogmatic beliefs about the primacy of one medium or the other that determines the relative proportions of speech and writing in the teaching, it is rather the effects of practical conditions and problems, such as for example weakness in the teacher's personal command of spoken language in some countries, or the existence of psycho-mechanical difficulties in teaching Roman script to children who have already learned Arabic script, and so on.

5. *The syllabus*

The teacher's activity is guided by the *syllabus*, a statement of content, sequence, and (often) recommended teaching techniques. (Sometimes the syllabus consists of an ordered list of grammatical items, together with a minimum vocabulary.) The choice of content for inclusion in the syllabus, and its arrangement, are exercised by the twin operations of *selection* and *grading* (p. 25). Both are nowadays carried out with more flexibility than in the past. A prior selection of language items to be taught is generally arrived at first, then this is integrated with an inventory of topics, roles, contexts and situations. In the most recent work, communicative abilities and even 'notional' categories of a semantico-grammatical kind are being included as determinants of the syllabus—but the more numerous the variables the more complex and difficult the job becomes (p. 107). That which is selected for teaching is regarded as a minimum, not a maximum, and is expected to be supplemented by much additional, unspecified and relatively uncontrolled material which the learner will meet in his reading and listening. Vocabulary lists and lists of word-frequencies are sometimes required (by educational authorities, not by the teachers) to be used, but they are regarded as e.g. checklists in the preparation of materials, not as rigid guidelines. Similarly, principles of grading have become looser. It is no longer believed that one would or should devise a sequence in which every teaching item had its immutable place. Rather it is believed that there are only a fairly small number of items (mostly grammatical) where it makes much difference whether you teach them early or late, or before or after other particular items; these sensitive items (which are often indicated by the common difficulties experienced by speakers of a particular language) are inserted in the sequence as required, but all other items are ideally allowed to occur at whatever point in sequence the topics, situations, etc. seem to suggest. This relaxed attitude to selection and grading provides much greater freedom in designing materials of interest and realism. It is an ideal which most forward-looking ESL authorities strive for, not least because it chimes with the imaginative experimentalism which teachers are encouraged to undertake. But it must be acknowledged that the older, more rigid attitudes to the syllabus are still widespread. As the newer, more flexible approach gains ground teachers find that it gives them relative independence in selecting content and interpreting the syllabus. The competent, confident, well-trained teacher welcomes this: the inadequate teacher fears it.

6. *Active and passive command*

From an early stage, a distinction is made between material (lexical or grammatical) which is taught for active command, to be recalled and used by the learner with facility and accuracy, and material which is to be recognized and understood when it is encountered but is not intended to be mastered. Recognition vocabulary is relatively uncontrolled, and stems from the imaginative use by the teacher or materials-writer of material designed to sustain and arouse the learner's interest. It can lie outside the confines of controlled vocabulary, grammar, etc., as long as the learner understands it when he meets it (even including apparent nonsense like Fee-fie-fo-fum or Rubadubdub or Jabberwocky. They, too, can be shown to be 'meaningful'.) More recent thought develops this receptive/productive distinction to embrace a distinction between *form* and *function*, so that it is not just the meaning of a sentence that is taught, but its value as an utterance. The absorption of substantial quantities of passive vocabulary is often achieved through quite ambitious, well-planned schemes of reading. On the productive side, a great deal of written work is set by the teacher, often as *homework*, which plays a big part (many would say, unfortunately) in British teaching.

7. *Techniques of presentation*

All class presentation is required to be *meaningful*. That is, the drilling of sentences regardless of whether they are understood or not is never attempted. (The term 'mim-mem' is known and rejected in British EFL; it is not generally known or understood in ESL.) Meaningful presentation is achieved by a mixture of techniques, especially these:

    (i) *contextualization*—suiting the action to the word, putting a word into a longer sentence, making clear the circumstances of its use, etc.;

    (ii) *explanation*—in either English or the mother tongue, including the occasional use of translation where this facilitates learning;

    (iii) *situational teaching*—the evocation of an event or a transaction (larger in scale than simple contextualization) in which the utterances are appropriate, e.g. by role-playing, playlets, puppet dialogues, games, and other contrived parallels to real-life situations.

Language material, meaningful and at least partly contextual, is presented under close control: *control* here means that the choice and timing of the piece of language concerned has been deliberate, even though this control may increasingly encourage the learner to encounter spoken or written language beyond that which he has mastered. Initially, the control is complete: the learner is completely spoon-fed by either the teacher or the materials. Later, both controlled and 'natural' material are presented. By the time the learner reaches the advanced stage he receives great quantities of natural (or only slightly-edited) language material. The control at that stage concentrates on areas of deficiency in the learner's knowledge, on forgetting, on error, or on deliberately-chosen new material. It is worth noting that in presenting material to the learner the teacher is trained to keep up the *pace* of learning. The watchword is, 'Don't just satisfy the learner, *stretch* him!'

8. *Grammar*

In British ELT, 'grammar' means not theoretical linguistics but part of the description of spoken and written English: it will be remembered that we have an exceptionally rich tradition of such studies. (The recent *Grammar of Contemporary English* by Quirk, Greenbaum, Leech and Svartik, well exemplifies this tradition.) The approach used in ELT generally follows the descriptive systems of Jespersen, Palmer and Hornby. Grammar is often referred to as *functional*, by which is meant that the statements we make are statements about the semantic and communicative significance of particular points of grammar, about how language is *used*, about the conveying of meaning or the maintenance of personal relations or the organization of discourse—about a number of inexplicit though relevant concepts of this kind.

Grammar is taught explicitly only if it is helpful to do so (for example, some learners *demand* to be taught grammar) and not as a dogma that good teaching does or does not require grammar to be made explicit. At the same time, grammar is not deliberately avoided. The amount of grammar taught depends on the age and previous experience of the learner, the stage of proficiency reached, the grammatical understanding of the teacher, and so on. There is a widespread use of inductive grammar teaching, in which sets of sentences are presented which embody a pattern and lead both to its accurate use and to its cognitive perception by the learner.

There is currently a wave of activity directed towards the revision of the treatment of grammar in syllabuses. This new work uses ideas about semantically-significant grammatical categories, communicative skills, functional and notional categories. It is likely that the results of this work, when it reaches teacher training courses, will considerably influence attitudes and practices.

9. *The teaching of reading and writing*

Reading is regarded as a skill of great importance to the learner, because (a) it provides him with access to a great quantity of further experience of the language, and (b) it gives him a window onto the normal means of continuing his personal education. Reading for content (i.e. for comprehension and to recover factual information) tends to be taught first; then comes reading for the deeper understanding of complex ideas, which is intellectual training as well as language practice; 'reading with one's ears' (e.g. for poetry) is also regarded as important by some teachers. A distinction is commonly made between *intensive* and *extensive* reading. Techniques for teaching the early stages of reading include both a *phonic* approach (in which the common phonetic values of letters are taught) and *look-and-say* methods (in which words are taught to be recognized by their total lexical shape).

As the learner progresses, he is generally introduced to structurally and lexically graded readers, which provide practice in reading and extend the learner's experience of the language without baffling him, and so turning off his learning, by too much lexical and stylistic unfamiliarity. It is regarded as important to get the young learner into the habit of reading as a normal part of his everyday life.

Writing, too, receives a great deal of attention. The teaching of writing entails at the outset control over elegant sequences of visual symbols. Here we are particularly proud of techniques based on the work of Marion Richardson, and we have developed ways of dealing with special problems where the learner has already learned a quite different script (Arabic, Devanagiri, Japanese, etc.). Then comes the production of ever longer and more intellectually complex sentences and texts: a graded progression from *tight control* through *guidance* to *free expression*.

Writing is taught at least partly for educational, rather than solely linguistic, reasons. By the time he reaches the advanced stages of learning English, the learner is exercising his powers of expression, persuasion, imagination, rhetoric, and using correct English as a vehicle for these achievements rather than as an end in itself. He is thus receiving, in his English teaching, 'training for judgment', as William Currie expresses it.

10. *Pronunciation*

The acquisition of an acceptable pronunciation is deliberately taught. Segmental sounds (phonemes in Daniel Jones' sense rather than

Bloomfield's), stress, rhythm and intonation are all included. Indeed, intonation is regarded as of high importance. There are several excellent textbooks which teach the main patterns of British intonation. Three main techniques are employed in the teaching of pronunciation:

(i) in the simplest and commonest cases, *pronunciation teaching* is by imitation and exhortation;

(ii) at a somewhat higher level, and more rarely, *speech training* makes use of exercises and games based on selected sounds, features or contrasts;

(iii) occasionally, with advanced learners and well-trained teachers, *practical phonetics* may be used (i.e. using phonetic transcription, articulation diagrams, ear training, technical exercises in the controlled production of sounds, etc.).

(These three techniques are described in greater detail in Chapter 7.)

The standards of pronunciation aimed at are flexible. Although the target towards which progress is assumed to lead is generally a non-regional accent of British English, in areas of the world where the educated community has developed an identifiably different yet compatible accent (e.g. Educated West African accent) this is often used as the aim and model. Intelligibility and communicative ability are the criteria (difficult though these are to define) rather than native-like quality.

There is virtually no bias in the British ELT profession against American, Australian and other native-language forms of English from outside Britain. Where there is an area of difficulty is when teachers with different forms of English teach the same class, or even teach in the same school. This problem has been made more obvious by the wide dispersion of Peace Corps volunteers in mainly British-English areas and British Voluntary Service Overseas personnel in mainly American-English areas. Even more serious is the low standard of spoken English among local teachers in some areas. Where money allows, this can be partly compensated for by the use of recordings. But in some areas it has become a serious question whether many teachers in fact have sufficient command of English to teach the spoken language at all.

11. *Practice material*

Exercises and drills of many kinds are used to fix the material presented and to achieve accurate, fluent, unhesitating command of the language. Their design and use is strictly pragmatic: they are not usually intended to demonstrate a psychological principle or to embody a theoretical concept for its own sake. They are intended to re-teach material already presented until the learner has already learned it: no more than that. For example, teachers are not governed by the principle that it is sufficient to concentrate on differences thrown up by contrastive analysis, leaving the similarities to look after themselves, and contrastive exercises or drills of such a kind play little part in British ESL teaching. The notion of 'overlearning' is generally rejected as a principle in the design of materials, at least in ESL. These attitudes reflect the kind of psychology commonly included in teacher training. Skinnerian behaviourist theory may be superficially known but is little followed; Lovell, Bruner, Burt, and above all Piaget, probably have greater influence.

Exercises are not devised in relation to a theory of language acquisition: teachers rarely have any organized view of such a theory, or if they do, they relate it to infants acquiring their mother tongue, not to teaching and learning a foreign language.

Exercises and drills are deliberately given the widest possible variety. A single technique is rarely assigned special prominence (e.g. pattern practice, substitution tables, etc.) though these techniques are used among many others. The offering of a wide range of different types of exercise is regarded as a virtue, and as a contribution to maintaining interest and fighting boredom. Mindless, boring drills are avoided.

12. *The search for interest*
Humour, variety, interesting material, demonstrably *relevant* material, involvement of the learner—especially relating the English course to the world of the learner outside the classroom—these are qualities deliberately sought because they are believed to improve both the rate of learning and the learner's continued commitment to the task.

13. *The teacher as an overseer of the learner's learning*
Teachers are trained in the belief that the learner should be regarded as the centre and focus of the entire teaching activity—though it must be admitted that many teachers frequently forget this. The learner's learning is to be continually assessed by the teacher, by informal and formal testing, by correcting exercises, by marking homework and by other means. The learner's communicative ability, the acceptability of his performance, the degree of his approximation to the appropriate model of language—these are criteria which the teacher spends a great deal of time and care in overseeing and assessing.

14. *The task of the teacher*
Though subsidiary to the learner, the teacher, too, is central to the language-teaching process. The teacher is relied upon for: (a) the presentation of material in an optimal manner; (b) the continuous, personal, long-term encouragement of the learner; (c) plugging the gaps in the learner's learning; (d) monitoring the learner's progress;

(e) remedial teaching, where this is necessary; (f) the selection and possibly the creation of materials supplementary to those centrally used by the class.

In achieving these aims, the teacher disposes of a wide array of teaching techniques among which he or she selects as the circumstances require. Ideally, the teacher is encouraged to slide along the scale between full-class techniques, group techniques, individual techniques.

The teacher faces a class: the class is composed of individuals: the individuals cluster as groups. The teacher's teaching techniques are intended from moment to moment to approach the ideal of helping each individual, as closely and as often as possible. The organization of group work within a large class is a feature of British classroom practice which is particularly valuable in ESL countries suffering, as many of them are, in the wake of massive educational expansion from very large classes. Perhaps this is why the American trend towards individualization has little counterpart among British teachers. Alternatively, the lack of interest in individualization among British teachers may reflect that fact that in ESL and EFL situations overseas teachers normally face classes that are much more homogeneous in nature than is the usual TEFL class in the United States.

Techniques are accepted if they give results, rejected if they don't. Thus, the *language laboratory* is seen as a potential aid to the teacher, given that (a) he possesses technical services to keep the equipment operational; (b) he has an understanding of its advantages and (particularly) its limitations; (c) he can obtain or produce suitable materials of use in the lab; and (d) he integrates lab work in some appropriate way into his courses as a whole, e.g. by pre- and post-lab sessions. Failing any of these pre-requisites, teachers tend to reject language labs as a waste of money. But at the same time, a good deal of thought is currently being given to ways of making lab work more interesting and effective. (See Chapter 13.)

The results of full contrastive analyses are only rarely sought, but some help is obtained from the fairly superficial study of common errors—a source of help that will be drawn on more systematically in the future. On the other hand, the teacher's experience is expected to lead him to identify and devise treatment for those learning difficulties that seem to stem from the learner's particular mother tongue, and also to be aware of different strategies employed by the learner, and to capitalize on these whenever possible.

15. *Teaching materials*
Teaching materials are relied on as aids to the teacher, not as panaceas or as ways of replacing the teacher. The best teachers use the materials as a general guide, but they take pride in transcending those materials—

68   Methodology and teacher training

cannibalizing them, improving on them, re-writing them, circumventing them, re-ordering or even omitting them—in the belief that the nub of the learning-teaching process lies in the moment-by-moment relationship between a competent teacher and a willing learner.

Equally, other aids such as flash cards, flannelgraphs, glove puppets, wall charts, pictures, slides, film strips, tapes, radio, television, films, language labs, etc., are regarded simply as *aids*. They are to be exploited by the teacher in the pursuit of excellence of learning, as and when they are available and relevant. They are not to be imposed upon the teacher or the learner, for reasons of dogma.

Conclusion

It is true, of course, that many of the points in the foregoing summary would be regarded as desirable by American as well as by British teachers. Equally, teachers both British and American would rightly claim that many of the points made are statements of the ideal rather than of what is always achieved. The summary may nevertheless be of some interest as a description of the main points of desirable practice in British ELT.

Acknowledgments

In preparing this chapter, I received great assistance from many friends, all of them language teaching specialists, who sent me their reactions to a draft of the summary of current British practice and methods. Many of them will recognize changes in the present text which reflect their comments. Imperfections remain, and these are my responsibility: for their help in avoiding the worst errors and exaggerations I express my sincere personal thanks to the following: Louis Alexander, Patrick Allen, W. Stannard Allen, Richard Allwright, Frank Bell, Geoffrey Broughton, Frank Brosnahan, Christopher Candlin, Guy Capelle, William Currie, June Derrick, Alan Davies, Richard Evans, Walter Grauberg, Michael Halliday, Richard Handscombe, David Harper, Eric Hawkins, Nicholas Hawkes, Roland Hindmarsh, A. S. Hornby, Arthur King, W. R. Lee, William F. Mackey, Ronald Mackin, Matthew Macmillan, Alan Moller, Ken Moody, Simon Murison-Bowie, Sirarpi Ohannessian, George Perren, John Spencer, David Stern, Gillian Sturtridge, Ray Tongue, John Webb, David Wilkins.

6 Some basic principles of teacher training

Introduction

Although there are a great many books and articles which deal with diffcrent aspects of the teaching of languages, there are few which concern themselves directly with the training of teachers as foreign-language specialists (including the teaching of English as a foreign or second language). This chapter attempts to summarize the nature of the teacher training task and to outline some of its underlying principles.

The Prime Elements of the Situation

The training of language teachers can be regarded as an attempt to produce the optimum 'match' or reconciliation between a number of disparate elements, whose precise nature varies from country to country, from one level of education to another, and according to a range of other factors. These 'prime elements' may be summarized thus:

1. *The personal attributes of the trainee.* His age, maturity, personality and temperament, intelligence, personal education, motivation for becoming a teacher, previous experience of children and adults, etc. All these will determine at least in part how successful the training will be and what sort of a teacher the trainee will become.

2. *The individual and group attributes of the pupils he will face.* The same course of training is not equally suitable for dealing with e.g., on the one hand, children of 7 years of age in a country overseas where English is a foreign language, and on the other, highly selected would-be university entrants of age 19, studying English intensively in Britain or the United States. Training is affected also by such factors as whether the teacher will be working in single-sex or mixed schools, by school traditions of discipline or indiscipline, by pupils' attitudes towards teachers and towards the learning of languages, etc.

3. *The nature of the educational process, of teaching in general and of language teaching in particular.* The trainee is entering a profession which has a long history and which has built up a substantial body of theory,

principle, practice and knowledge, both about the general notion of how to promote the education of a human being and about the special problems of doing this in relation to particular subjects. The training he will receive takes account of this body of thought.

4. *The target situation for which the trainee is being trained.* It is rare for a trainee not to have a fairly close idea of the educational level at which he is preparing to teach, and of other basic features of the job he expects to take up. As a rule, training courses concentrate on a particular age-group, type of school, etc., or at least they differentiate between the main possibilities so that the trainee is prepared as closely as possible for the kind of school, kind of class, kind of learner, kind of teaching, in which he will ultimately find himself working after he completes his training.

5. *The realistic possibilities of training.* A further element which the foregoing must match, and be matched to, reflects the shortcomings and constraints of the training operation. Is there sufficient time for the course to impart all the trainee needs? Is the staff of the training college or university department of sufficient quality and standard? Are there a sufficient number of them? Are there adequate facilities, books, equipment, etc., in the training institution? Can suitable arrangements be made for supervised practice teaching? Are teacher trainers (and teachers) adequately paid, and do they enjoy a high status in the community? These and other questions delimit the realistic possibilities of teacher training in a given instance.

These prime elements are not themselves the components of a teacher training course. They are, rather, the variables which have to be reconciled in order to make possible any teacher training course which satisfies minimum criteria of adequacy and appropriateness. It is possible to conceive in the abstract a number of alternative ways in which this reconciliation might be brought about. But in reality there has evolved (in the British tradition, at least) an approach which postulates the characteristics of the 'ideal' teacher and proposes a scheme for attaining an ideal; at the same time it recognizes that there are limitations in practice which prevent the ideal from being attained, and it offers a rule-of-thumb guide to the priority of different elements in the ideal programme, according to the main impediments and constraints that occur.

The Characteristics of the 'Ideal' Language Teacher

Few of those engaged in training teachers would conceive of a teacher who would be 'ideal' for all and any teaching circumstances. The art and craft of teaching is so diverse and varied that no such paragon would be likely to exist. What is possible, however, is to conceive of an ideal which is re-defined in terms of the particular kinds of teaching situation he or she actually proposes to engage in. Such an ideal would possess *personal qualities, technical abilities* and *professional understanding* of the following kinds:

1. *Personal qualities.* These include both inherent qualities and other qualities acquired through experience, education or training. Among the former we must recognize physical and psychological attributes. It is obvious (but needs stating) that physical handicaps and deformities— e.g., blindness, startling scars, gross size or smallness or other stigmata that might be traumatic to children or adults—are likely to interfere with the teaching/learning relationship. Equally, it is obvious (but needs stating) that the teacher must be intelligent, have a 'non-discouraging personality', and display emotional maturity. Among the acquired qualities are to be included a wide experience of life, an adequate level of personal education (the educator must be seen to be educated), and a sufficient command of the language he is teaching. (The question of how great is a 'sufficient command' of the language is a difficult one to answer. My own preference is to define it as 'error-free in the classroom', leaving out of judgment any greater command that the teacher may display in his private life. This is a minimum, but it is at least more capable of being achieved than many broader statements of ability.)

2. *Technical abilities.* These are of three kinds: first, ability to discern and assess the progress and difficulties of his pupils; an unhesitating control of the teaching in his classes so as to maximize the rate of learning; secondly, a fluent and responsive grasp of classroom skills and techniques; and thirdly, a 'creative familiarity' with the syllabus and materials being used in his classes, such that he can improve on them as occasion demands by devising his own material.

3. *Professional understanding.* This refers to a sense of perspective that sees the teacher's own particular task in relation to all types of language learning/teaching situation, to an awareness of trends and developments in language teaching, and to an acceptance that it is his professional duty to go on improving his professional effectiveness throughout his career.

A Scheme for Training Teachers Towards the Ideal

Most teacher training courses contain four basic elements:
1. *Selection,* both initially, for acceptance as a trainee, and terminally, for acceptance as a teacher.
2. *Continuing personal education of the trainee.*
3. *General professional training as an educator and teacher.*
4. *Special training as a teacher of a foreign or second language.*
Each of these elements deserves further discussion.

1. *Selection.* Not every human being would make an adequate teacher, let alone a good one. To say this is not necesssarily to embrace the slogan that 'good teachers are born, not made'. But just as some individuals quickly mark themselves out during training as likely to become teachers of outstanding effectiveness, so also a small number of individuals mark themselves out as unsuitable for the profession. The latter category includes not only those obviously disqualified by handicap or defect, but others whose personalities or attitudes run counter to those which the collective experience of educators regards as necessary or acceptable. Most of these can be identified at the time they apply to be accepted for teacher training; others are only identified in the course of training—for example, those who unexpectedly find themselves terrified by the experience of facing a class of learners. Each member of the teaching profession bears an important and continuing responsibility, throughout a career which may last for thirty years or longer, towards the individuals who make up his classes. This responsibility makes it essential that potentially damaging or ineffective individuals should be discouraged from entering the profession, by adequate pre-training or post-training selection procedures.

2. *Continuing personal education.* The fundamental principle is obvious: teachers should not be ill-educated people. But the minimum standards of education commonly and publicly accepted for teachers in particular kinds of institution vary from country to country and may change as a result of major social and political developments. There are variations, too, in how the trainee's personal education is improved: either simultaneously with his professional training, as in British colleges of education and in many countries where a degree in education incorporates 'general studies'; or consecutively, as in British universities, where (typically) a non-vocational three-year degree, with no element of training as a teacher, is followed by a one-year postgraduate course of teacher training; or, as in several countries, by in-service courses of various kinds. Either way, the assumption remains that a simple school-leaver's level of education is to be regarded as insufficient for a teacher.

3. *General professional training as an educator and teacher.* This element embraces that which *all* teachers need to know, understand, do and hope for, regardless of whether they will be teachers of general subjects or specialists in mathematics, history, the mother tongue, or a foreign language. The training given generally embraces the following:

  (a) A component intended to guide the trainee towards an understanding of the nature of education in relation to the individual and to society. This component usually includes educational psychology, the study of child development, some social psychology, and the principles of educational thought.

(b) An outline of the organization of education in the country concerned, so that the teacher is aware of the different kinds of school and other institution; of normal and unusual pathways through the educational network; of chains of responsibility, control and finance; of sources of reform and change; of the main features of the history of education in the country where he will be teaching.

(c) An awareness of the moral and 'rhetorical' function of the teacher: the building of standards, character, enthusiasm. (There is a tendency within language teaching for some teachers to reject this responsibility and to regard themselves as concerned solely with imparting language ability. This rejection seems to me to be based on a misconception. Whether he likes it or not, the teacher *is* a model and exemplar, the texts he chooses *are* culturally loaded, his own outlook *must* intrude into his teaching. That is quite different from saying that the teaching has to promote the values of a particular culture: the teacher has a choice of outlooks and attitudes. But it is almost impossible to be totally neutral, since he is a human being engaged in interaction with other human beings.)

(d) Knowledge of, and skill in, class management, discipline, and the handling of large and small numbers of pupils.

(e) Knowledge of, and skill in, basic instructional techniques, and an understanding of the interaction between teacher and learner.

(f) Acceptance of the absolute, fundamental need for the preparation of lessons, so that the teacher *never* goes into the classroom without having a clear intention of teaching some specific item or material, in a particular way.

(g) Understanding the role and inter-relationships of curriculum, syllabus and teaching materials.

(h) A commitment on the part of the teacher to keep abreast of developments in the profession of teaching.

4. *Special training as a teacher of a foreign or second language.* The considerable quantity and complexity of this training, which in fact constitutes the core of most teacher training courses, can be rendered more simple if a distinction is made between three rather different aspects of it, which for convenience we shall label the 'skills' component, the 'information' component and the 'theory' component. The main differences between these aspects are on the whole self-evident, but are not watertight compartments, and some parts of a training course may not easily fit into one of these categories rather than another.

(i) *The SKILLS Component*
Three different kinds of skills are required of the teacher:

(a) *Command of the language he or she is teaching.* The teacher of a language is the learner's model, especially as far as the spoken language is concerned, and if the teacher's command of the language is inadequate, the learner's achievements will be impaired. Learners, including children, have a pretty good general idea of their teacher's standard, even though they themselves may be complete beginners. It is a source of great discouragement (and therefore a constraint upon learning) for a learner to have a teacher whose command of the language is inadequate, who makes obvious errors in the classroom, who is uncertain about meanings and grammatical patterns, who has no confidence in his own grasp of the language. Consequently the skills component of a teacher training course must ensure that the teacher's command of English (or whatever language he is teaching) is at least adequate for classroom purposes. *This ought to be a make-or-break requirement,* since the teacher without an adequate command of the language is probably wasting his own time and that of all his pupils, and he may be bruising their general enthusiasm as learners into the bargain.

(b) *Teaching techniques and classroom activities.* It is not self-evident to the trainee how 'a language' can be broken down into teachable items, nor how these may best be presented so that their significance is grasped and the learner is enabled to use them with accuracy and ease. Yet a great body of ingenious and effective techniques does exist and it is a major part of his training to imbibe and assimilate this collective professional experience.

(c) *The 'management of learning'.* Not every act of teaching is immediately effective. Sometimes a point is grasped by some learners in a class but not by others. Individuals in a class learn more readily or rapidly than others, and display personal differences in learning of the kinds discussed in Chapter 4. Sometimes an individual enters a period of faster learning, or goes through a patch of poor learning. It is a crucial part of the teacher's classroom skills to learn how to assess from moment to moment the progress of each individual in the class, and how to manage the classroom activity so that the fastest and most able learners are not frustrated by being held back, while the slowest learners are not depressed by being left behind. This management of learning is one of the most subtle and difficult skills to acquire, needing both experience of observing a good teacher exercising the skill and the opportunity to see the problem in a class of his own while still in a position to be advised on how to cope with it. This raises the vital question of how the practical skills of teaching are best taught to the trainee teacher: a separate section of this chapter is devoted to that topic later.

(ii) *The INFORMATION Component*

There is a great deal that the teacher needs to *know*, which he would not need to know if he were not a language teacher. The body of information can be sub-divided into three parts:

(a) *Information about education*, about different approaches to the task of teaching the language, about methodology. This knowledge is no substitute for the skill of being able to teach, but it offers the teacher an intellectual basis for what he is doing. The more sophisticated and the better-educated the trainee, the more he is likely to feel a need for this cognitive base to his skill.

(b) *Information about the syllabus and materials* he will be using. In a sense, the syllabus, the prescribed textbooks, the ancillary materials (readers, workbooks, etc.) and the available aids (flashcards, puppets, wall-charts, etc. as well as hardware such as tape recorders and language labs) make up the tools of the teacher's trade. Few kinds of information are of more direct help to the trainee than familiarity with these tools of the trade, acquired before he first goes into his own classroom as a fully-fledged teacher.

(c) *Information about language*. It needs to be remembered that when a teacher enters his course of training, his understanding of the nature of language, and therefore of the very concept with which his whole career will be concerned, is likely to be scanty. It may even be compounded of folklore and confusion (e.g. 'the sounds of letters'; 'English has no grammar'; 'Some languages are better/more beautiful than others', etc.). There are few countries as yet where the education of the young adult contains much information or understanding of the kind which is essential to the language teacher. What kind of information are we referring to? To knowledge of which the following is a brief selection: differences between animal communication systems and human language; normal stages in the infant's acquisition of his mother tongue; the impediment of deafness; the existence of common speech defects and whose job it is to treat them; relations between speech and writing; literacy and education; notions of 'correctness' and social judgments on language; language variety, including dialects and accents; the reflection of a people's history in its language; languages in contact; artificial languages; language and thought; language and logic; language and literature; and many more. This body of knowledge is sometimes called 'an introduction to the study of language', a study distinct from, though related to, the scientific discipline of linguistics. We shall return to this distinction later; for the moment the point being made is that teacher training courses ideally contain a section of information about language. Also within this section would be included some acquaintance with descriptions of the language being taught and of the pupils' mother tongue. In the case of training teachers of English, there exists a rich tradition of the description of English presented for the use of the teacher, from Sweet, through Jespersen, Palmer and Hornby, flowering most recently in the *Grammar of Contemporary English*, by Quirk, Greenbaum, Leech and Svartvik. The teacher should have some familiarity with a description of the language he is going to teach, preferably a description whose terms are compatible with the description inherent in the syllabus he will be teaching.

(iii) *The THEORY Component*

At its most sophisticated, the language teaching profession makes connections with rigorous theoretical studies in several disciplines, notably in *linguistics, psychology, psycholinguistics, sociolinguistics, social theory, education.* There is, however, an unfortunate ambiguity about the word *theory* which often makes for futile arguments as to what 'theoretical' studies should and could be incorporated in teacher training courses. In the tradition of the humanities, 'theory' commonly means 'generalization', 'principle' or 'abstraction', but makes no stipulation about how such notions have been reached. In this weaker sense of the word 'theory' there need be little disagreement that all teacher training courses should include a theory component, through which the trainee could hope to acquire an understanding of his actions and their effects. Theory in this sense provides the 'why' of language teaching, allied to the 'what' of the information component and the 'how' of the skills.

But there is a stronger, more rigorous meaning of 'theory': when it is used in the scientific tradition, 'theory' means a body of abstractions which has been arrived at by certain specified steps and which bears a quite specific relation to 'data' and to observed facts. Both linguistics and psychology are sciences in this sense and use the term *theory* in a rigorously defined way. So to reach an understanding of *theoretical* linguistics and *theoretical* psychology requires a high level of intellectual training, which in turn entails a relatively long period of study and a high standard of teaching. Yet the direct gain to the language teacher which these theoretical studies provide is often rather small. In this rigorous sense of 'theory', then, it is only when the trainee has attained a sufficient level of personal education and when the training course has sufficient time available to justify its inclusion, and when he is preparing to teach high-level learners, that theoretical studies are likely to find a place. Such conditions do exist: the experienced graduate teacher, returning to the university for further studies, for example, may well find considerable benefit from a theoretical element in his training.

An alternative plan, commonly followed in Britain, is to include as the 'theoretical' component in postgraduate teacher training the inter-disciplinary approach of *applied linguistics*, which, as we saw in Chapter 3, integrates appropriate parts of the disciplines most relevant to language teaching. Applied linguistics in this sense mediates between the theoretical and the practical. The applied linguist needs to be aware of developments in theory as well as of practical problems, so that he can use insights from the former to assist the latter—and sometimes vice versa. Out of such studies there is currently emerging a theoretical view of the total language learning and teaching process, a 'theory of language teaching' which will doubtless contribute more directly to future teacher training than linguistics or psychology have been able to do as separate disciplines.

Before leaving the three basic components of teacher training courses we should note that the imparting of them requires different procedures. The *information* content can be learned from reading, from lectures or other techniques of the kind; relatively little discussion is required. The *theory* component can only rarely be assimilated in that way: discussion, practice in solving problems, tutorial explanations, and sheer time to absorb new habits of thought, are all necessary. The *skills* component requires practical training in actually performing the skills themselves.

Practical Training of the Skills Element

Teacher trainers have devoted decades of intelligence, ingenuity and experience to the development of practical training in teaching, and a great range of different activities are current. They can be roughly summarized as follows:

(i) The observation of specially-devised demonstrations, both of specific techniques and of complete lessons.

(ii) The observation of actual classes.

(iii) Practice in the preparation of lesson plans for various contingencies.

(iv) Micro-teaching: the teaching (by the trainee) of specific items or techniques, possibly with the use of closed-circuit television and videotape recordings.

  (v) Peer-group teaching (i.e. teaching fellow-trainees) as a form of exercise.
  (vi) Acting as teacher's assistant in a genuine class.
  (vii) Teaching real classes under supervision.
  (viii) Post-mortem criticism and discussion of the trainee's teaching.
  (ix) Longer-term apprenticeship in a school, with attachment to an experienced teacher.
  (x) Post-training, in-service courses of various kinds.

Training is a highly complex activity which requires knowledge, understanding, practice and experience before it can be carried out in a fully professional and effective manner: the trainee progresses towards these goals through the information, theory and skills components of his training.

Differences Between Teacher Training Courses

Not all teacher training courses start from the same point in attempting to produce the optimum mix of the prime elements; nor are the aims the same in all cases. The principal sources of difference between different training courses are these:

  (a) *Time available.* Some training courses may last only two or three weeks; others may last four years or more. There are differences, too, in the *intensity* of courses, as well as in their *duration*.
  (b) *The target situations for which teachers are being trained.* This includes levels of education (primary, secondary, etc.), whether the pupils will be selected or non-selected, homogeneous or mixed, and so on.
  (c) *The educational standard and emotional maturity of the trainees.* Training 16-year-old school leavers and training 25-year-old ex-servicemen are very different tasks.
  (d) *The staff and facilities available.* Training institutions vary in the calibre of their staff, and in the extent to which the numbers of good people they employ are sufficient for the volume of training they undertake. Some colleges have better libraries than others. Similarly, there are major differences in the availability of facilities for demonstration and practice teaching. Shortcomings in staff affect the quality of the *theory* component most of all; shortcomings in library holdings affect the *information* component; shortcomings in demonstration and practice facilities affect the *skills* component.

Response to Shortcomings

As a broad generalization one may say that the proportions of the three components of a particular teacher training course are decided as a response to the fundamental variables of *time available, trainee educational level* and *target teaching level* (e.g. primary, secondary, university, etc.). The longer the time available, the higher the trainee educational level, and the higher the target teaching level, the greater is the proportion of time given to theory and information relative to skills; and conversely. Hence a short course indicates a preponderance of time spent on skills; so does a lower target teaching level, such as training for primary school work; so also does a lower educational level on the part of the trainee.

Justification—or Excuse?

There is a danger that the very real practical need for a restriction on 'theory' components, at least in the more academic interpretation of the term, because of shortage of time, may be used as an excuse and a cover for anti-intellectual attitudes. Many teacher-trainers regard statements of the kind 'We concentrate on practical teaching—none of this theoretical nonsense!' as if they were robust common sense, when in fact such slogans display short-sighted obscurantism.

It probably *is* true that very little transformational-generative theory, or stratificational theory, or systemic theory, or case grammar, could be thoroughly taught and learned during, say, a two-year training college course. The reasons for this include the following: (a) the intellectual rigour of theoretical studies in linguistics requires a high standard of prior mental training which students at this level have rarely had the opportunity to acquire; (b) the number of hours that need to be devoted to such studies is rather large; (c) the number of college lecturing staff with a suitable background for teaching such students is rather small; and (d) the relevance of such studies to the trainee's future work is inversely related to the educational level at which they will work: the lower down the system, the less relevant.

Theory Component in Short Courses

Against these arguments, however, can be set the following: first, the purpose of the 'theory' element in teacher training is to provide *understanding*, as distinct from *knowledge*, and understanding is not a component that can be dispensed with in training for a profession, especially within the field of education; second, theoretical courses in academic subjects, organized in forms suitable for university degree work, are not necessarily the best way of helping trainee teachers to achieve understanding; and third, among the alternatives to full-scale theoretical courses is a range of alternatives falling under the general heading of *applied linguistics*, which, as we saw in Chapter 3, provides ready-made packages containing the appropriate parts of the relevant disciplines, specially adapted to mediate between the practical and the theoretical. In other words, the theory component *can* be provided, even on short courses, by suitably tailored versions of the multi-disciplinary approach of applied linguistics. Evidence that this can be done is provided by courses such as the ten-week Certificate in Applied Linguistics and the Teaching of English (CALTE) of the University of Essex, within which a considerable depth of understanding—i.e. the aim of the 'theory' component of teacher training—is achieved in a single term's course.

The preceding outline attempts to relate the principal variables underlying all teacher training. Before closing this chapter, one further commonly held view needs to be added. Teacher trainers are generally convinced that their work is *dynamic*, not *static*, and that teacher training courses need to be re-assessed from time to time and brought into line with current developments in the contributing disciplines.

7 Teaching the spoken language: phonetics, speech training and pronunciation teaching

The problems of *teaching* pronunciation are often confused with the problems of *learning* pronunciation. It is sometimes difficult to be certain how far the learning is the result of the teaching: in the realm of pronunciation the inter-relations between learning and teaching are intricately entwined. Every word, every syllable, every phoneme uttered by the teacher may contribute to the learner's learning of pronunciation, not only when the teacher is deliberately and overtly concentrating on teaching pronunciation but equally when the teacher believes he is putting the weight of his teaching on to questions of grammar or vocabulary, or when he is simply easing the class along by an exchange of greetings, or telling a little story.

Pronunciation is the sector of language where the organization of syntax and semantics, having first been generated in the brain as a series of solely *mental* processes—silent, instantaneous, electrical and chemical—is converted into *motor* activity, which in turn produces acoustic effect, i.e. audible sounds. The immensely delicate link between brain and muscles sets pronunciation apart from all other facets of language except writing, which in the case of alphabetic systems normally requires prior mastery of pronunciation before it can in turn be mastered. Any human actions that are psycho-*motor* in nature, rather than solely *mental*, are by definition subject to the limitations which apply to all muscular training. In a sense—though this is an over-simplification—teaching pronunciation is more like *gymnastics* than *linguistics*.

The foregoing is a summary of some of the reasons why teachers of a second or foreign language find that their pupils face special learning difficulties in pronunciation, and why teachers themselves need a separate rationale to guide them in teaching it.

A rationale for the teaching of pronunciation consists of a reasoned, principled attempt to match the *learner* (as an individual, defined by his personal profile of learning abilities) with appropriate *teaching* (selected from the total range of possible teaching techniques). We have already seen in Chapter 4 that different learners display variations in their

language learning ability: in the particular instance of learning pronunciation, two of what were earlier called the learner's static qualities are of especial importance. They are:
(i) *age*, and (ii) *'a good ear'*

(i) *Age and ability in pronunciation learning*
There are both advantages and disadvantages in growing older. The principal disadvantages seem to be these:

(a) *Reduced auditory discrimination*. With the acquisition of the sound patterns of our first language it may be that the need for close auditory discrimination is reduced and the ability itself declines. However, it can be revived, even in adults, by specialized training: the reduction in the ability to distinguish sounds, which generally takes place as the individual grows older, is not irreversible.

(b) *Inferior self-monitoring*. As we grow older we pay more attention to *what* we say, and less to the phonetic detail of *how* we actually say it, which we increasingly take for granted. In learning a foreign language this becomes something of a disadvantage, though once again, as with auditory discrimination, it can be compensated for, by training.

(c) *Reduced power of mimicry*. A few individuals retain into adulthood the ability to mimic any speech they hear, including subtle features of accent. But the majority lose this power, and require much practice in order to revive it sufficiently for the purposes of language learning.

(d) *Increased shyness*. Most individuals become unwilling to make unfamiliar sounds, or to run the risk of committing errors of performance, in front of other people.

(e) *Greater reliance on writing*. The learner who is already literate in his mother tongue is likely to become increasingly dominated by the *written* form of language, rather than by *speech*.

(ii) *Possession of a 'good ear'*
Apart from changes that accompany ageing, individuals *at a given age* vary in their possession of a set of abilities, rarely analysed but often referred to as 'a good ear for languages'. A learner who possesses this advantage usually has a mixture of above-average hearing, auditory discrimination and powers of mimicry, with heightened interest in language and willingness to learn particular languages. Differences of this kind between individuals are more obvious among adults than among young children.

But in addition to the disadvantages outlined above, adults also possess countervailing advantages in learning pronunciation. Some of these we have already noted in connection with learning languages in general, others are specific to this sector of language:

(a) *The adult has learned how to learn*, so that he can, if he wishes, take more learning benefit from each hour of teaching than the child can.

(b) *The adult has greater powers of deliberate concentration* on any given task, and his attention-span is much longer.

(c) *The adult has less need for inherent interest in the teaching materials*, whereas the child's motivation has to be maintained by variety, amusement, and subterfuge.

(d) *The adult can follow detailed instructions* and can intellectualize his learning, for example by applying general rules, by learning about the organs of speech, by understanding that sounds in isolation are related to meaningful language, or by the use of phonetic symbols, etc. For example, an adult having learned about the nature and function of the soft palate and its connection with nasality, he can subsequently control the nasal-oral distinction in his own speech by deliberate movement of his organs of speech.

(e) In some cases, *the adult has greater experience of learning other foreign languages.*

If we turn from the qualities of the individual learner to consideration of a general process, it seems to be the case that when learners, exercising the qualities and abilities which we have been analysing, encounter the sounds of a foreign language and start to learn to pronounce it accurately, a good deal of their learning is reasonably successful, irrespective of the precise teaching techniques employed.

The majority of sound features are imitated with reasonable accuracy by the majority of learners, without special teaching. This inherent efficiency of pronunciation learning is perhaps not altogether surprising. The total possible range of phonetic items and systems in all human languages is fairly small, and the degree of overlap between languages is quite large; consequently many sounds are broadly familiar to the learner and present a zero learning load, and his powers of mimicry can be concentrated on a smaller target than 'the whole of' the phonetic and phonological system. As the learner grows older the proportion of sounds he can deal with in this automatic fashion generally declines from, say 80% at age 10 to 70% at age 25. It is of course arbitrary to assign a precise figure to the proportion of the sounds an individual manages to learn to pronounce without conscious effort and by sheer mimicry. But it is common experience that *most* learners learn *most* sounds in this way, and that the basic problem of teaching pronunciation is concentrated on, first, the residual sounds that most pupils find difficult, and second, the residual pupils who find most sounds difficult.

These observations lead us to the first of two major principles about learning pronunciation, which will inform our rationale for teaching it.

Principle No. 1

Most learners will learn to produce most sound features of a foreign language with reasonable accuracy by mimicry alone, given the opportunity; this ability tends to decrease somewhat with age.

Next we should consider the main range of teaching techniques which can be invoked to assist pupils in learning pronunciation. They are of three basic and distinct kinds:

(i) *exhortation*, that is, instructions to imitate and mimic, to make such and such a sound, without further explanation;

(ii) *speech training*, the construction of special games and exercises which entail the use of words or sentences so as to practise particular sounds, sequences of sounds, stress-patterns, rhythm, intonation, etc.;

(iii) *practical phonetics*, including especially the following:
    (a) description of the organs of speech
    (b) description of the articulation of sounds
    (c) description of stress, rhythm and intonation
    (d) ear training (i.e. practice in auditory discrimination)
    (e) production exercises (i.e. practice in actually making particular sounds, both in words and sentences, and in isolation, and in 'nonsense' sequences).

These three techniques were listed in ascending order of sophistication, from the standpoint of pupil and teacher alike.

Exhortation requires no special training on the part of the teacher and no special understanding on the part of the learner. 'No, Anna: not *dis*; *this*. Say *this*. *This*. Again: *this*. Good girl!' We all use this technique all the time, and it works pretty well.

Speech training is a more deliberately-organized technique. The teacher who introduces a sentence like *These three trees are green* to practise the differences between *th-* in *these* and *th-* in *three*, or to practise the vowel in *three*, is engaged in an elementary form of speech training. Given some ingenuity and imagination and an understanding of the phonetic and phonological facts of English, a good teacher can give the class a good deal of enjoyment while deliberately teaching special points of pronunciation.

Phonetics requires prior professional training and also demands something rather different, almost intellectual, of the learner.

It would be misleading to suggest that there are watertight divisions between exhortation and mimicry, speech training and phonetics, especially since the best results are obtained by the teacher who can call on the particular mixture of techniques that the precise moment requires. There is nevertheless a sense in which the three techniques represent an ascending order of sophistication and intellectualization, for both learner and teacher; the more an individual learner possesses the full range of possible advantages of the adult, the more easily he can benefit from greater sophistication in the teaching techniques that are employed upon him.

A second major principle about learning pronunciation emerges:

Principle No. 2

Older learners can take more benefit than younger learners from formal, specialized, intellectualized teaching methods; the more sophisticated the learner, the more sophisticated the instruction that can be used upon him, and the greater the standard of achievement per hour of instruction he will typically reach.

This principle is concerned with techniques of learning and teaching which clearly depend for their success on considerable special experience and prior training for both learner and teacher.

We are now in a position to suggest a rationale for the teaching of pronunciation, based on the two principles put forward above. Before doing so, it may be worth explaining why it is a rationale that is proposed—i.e. a basis for practical action—and not a 'theory of pronunciation teaching'.

One reason lies in the nature of theory-building. The statements we have made about pronunciation learning and teaching, and the justifications put forward for them, are not capable of being formalized or reduced to symbols in ways that would be necessary before the term 'theory' became appropriate in its full rigour. But a second and more decisive reason is that we are here dealing with the interface or connection between two activities of very different kinds.

Teaching is an art: language is a special case of the general category of teaching; pronunciation teaching is a yet further special case of the category of language teaching. It may be that in our proper respect for theories as a whole, and scientific theories of the most rigorous kind in particular, we have confused the places in our professional activities as language teachers where specific types of intellectual concept belong. Language teaching is one task: establishing linguistic theory is another. Linguistic theory is a source of reference and a fount of ideas and of illumination about language, it requires cerebral training which can benefit the understanding of every language teacher. But we have perhaps been too anxious in the past to transfer scientific theory into the realm of the pedagogical art without the transmogrification, the transmutation, that is essential when moving from one universe of discourse to another. There exists a phonetic theory, and at least one phonological theory, and several theoretical statements about the relation between phonology and syntax or grammar. But for the purpose of establishing the most appropriate teaching methods and techniques for teaching pronunciation to a given group of learners it is not a theory that is required, but simply a rationale—a set of justified reasons for selecting an appropriate course of action.

A rationale for pronunciation teaching

1. The target or model of pronunciation to be learned must be consciously selected and terminal standards of achievement must be formulated, not only in general terms ('adequate intelligibility', 'native-like accent', etc.) but as precisely as possible.

2. The most effective teaching approach takes account of the individual learner and of his learning ability in relation to his age and to his degree of sophistication as a language learner.

3. Exhortation, imitation and mimicry will take care of a large portion of the pronunciation learning task, and these techniques should normally be used first, regardless of the age of the learner. They have the advantage of requiring little or no specialized training on the part of the teacher.

4. Remaining problems in learning pronunciation should be tackled through the use of teaching techniques as far along the lines of sophistication (i.e. from exhortation at one end through speech training to the use of practical phonetics at the other) as the learner's own sophistication, and the specialized training of the teacher, permit.

5. As a general guide, young learners will learn best through mimicry with speech training games for interest and for special points of difficulty, but with little or no use of phonetics; linguistically-sophisticated adults can profit more easily from phonetics, particularly from the deliberate use of drills and exercises in practical ear training and phonetics.

6. Teachers should receive sufficient specialized training to enable them to apply the maximum sophistication of pronunciation-teaching technique that is suitable for the age of their learners.

To sum up the argument of this chapter, people who learn a second or foreign language *can* learn good pronunciation, at any age. They will *actually* do so in a higher proportion of cases and with greater effectiveness, if the teaching to which they are exposed takes account both of the principle that most people learn most of the elements of pronunciation easily, and of the other principle, that for residual problems it pays the teacher to be as sophisticated as the learners can take.

Part Three

Special Problems in ELT

8 The teaching of English for special purposes

When discussing alternative possible educational perspectives for language teaching (Chapter 2, p. 19) we noticed that there has been a major change in recent years, away from the earlier assumption of language teaching as a handmaiden of literary studies, first towards a conception of teaching and learning the practical command of a language, unrelated to aspects of culture, and more recently towards the notion that the teaching of a language can with advantage be deliberately matched to the specific needs and purposes of the learner.

The name 'English for Special Purposes' (ESP) is usually given to this kind of course, and it is generally used in circumstances in which the command of English being imparted relates to a specific job, or subject, or purpose. To offer such courses at all is a break with the long tradition of English as part of a general education; to offer them in relation to science or technology suggests a potential conflict with the assumption that English belongs in the humanities and is allied above all to the study of literature. ESP is growing at a great pace. The demand for immediate action—that is, for special syllabuses to be prepared, special materials to be written, and staff to be recruited who will teach to these specialized goals—has outstripped the time needed for such major developments to be accommodated and assimilated by the profession. Consequently many inadequate courses are being taught, by teachers who are unsure of how they should proceed, while at the same time the essential development work is being urgently pursued in the hope of catching up with the demand before too much damage is done by unsatisfactory responses to the demand for immediate action.

We shall concentrate on three aspects of ESP: first, on the great diversity of courses which come under the general heading of ESP. We shall suggest an analysis and classification (i.e. a taxonomy) of such courses, as a way of recognizing the main kinds of decision that need to be taken by those responsible for preparing courses. Second, we shall look briefly at the nature of 'Scientific English'. Third, we shall consider in some detail the implications of the principle, now almost universally accepted but rarely explained, that ESP should be concerned with the 'communicative purposes' of the learner.

1. A Taxonomy of ESP

In this analysis, it is proposed that all ESP courses can be sub-divided into a number of different types, some of which need to be further divided; and that all ESP courses, of all types, are subject to two 'pedagogical dimensions'.

What is to be included, and what excluded, under the heading 'ESP'? Broadly defined, ESP courses are those in which the aims and the content are determined, principally or wholly, not by criteria of general education (as when 'English' is a foreign language subject in school) but by functional and practical English language requirements of the learner.

English courses for medical doctors, for meteorologists, for secretaries, for business men, for diplomats, for welders, for air traffic controllers, for nurses, for chemical engineers, for students of physics or English literature, for teachers or teacher trainers—all these, and many more, are examples of ESP.

Within ESP, a crucial distinction exists between courses of 'English for Science and Technology' (EST), and all other courses. EST courses are usually distinct because they require the incorporation within them of a greater content of 'scientific English'. This in turn entails the learning of ways in which quantification of various kinds is expressed in English, the control of the 'international' vocabulary of scientific stems and affixes as they operate in English, and the selection of communicative purposes special to science and technology. We shall return later to the nature of 'scientific English'. In the meantime, the first and basic distinction within ESP is between (i) *EST* and (ii) *all other ESP*.

A second set of distinctions also applies within all ESP, and that is between (i) *occupational*, and (ii) *educational* courses. As the name implies, occupational ESP relates to a job, occupation or profession, as for example courses in English for fire-fighters, meteorologists, airline cabin staff, or teachers. In all types of occupational ESP a distinction emerges between *pre-experience* and *post-experience* courses, depending on whether the learner is already familiar with the job and is simply adding a relevant knowledge of English, or whether the English for the job is being taught at the same time as he or she is learning the job itself. As far as teachers are concerned, occupational ESP already offers conversion or re-training courses of a kind sometimes called 're-tread courses' (by analogy with the process of putting a fresh pattern of tread on a motor-car tyre), in which people already trained as teachers of some other language, e.g. French, are enabled to convert to teaching English in addition, or instead. *Occupational ESP*, then, sub-divides into *pre-experience*, *post-experience* and teachers' *conversion* courses.

Educational ESP varies according to its educational aims and the framework (particularly the level) within which it is offered. In higher education, 'English for academic purposes' can be said to relate to the study of a discipline, e.g. physics, chemical engineering, tropical agriculture, literary criticism. *Discipline-based* ESP is much affected by the question of whether the students concerned have already completed their study of the discipline or whether they are learning English as part of their studies: these different types might be labelled *pre-study* and *in-study* ESP. One very numerous body of overseas students in Britain, often referred to as 'pre-technical students', consists of those who are learning English specifically in order to gain admission to a course in science or technology: for such students, ESP needs to include a major component of study skills.

School subject ESP, although rare, is increasingly offered. Here it is necessary to distinguish between *independent* and *integrated* ESP courses: in the former, the English is offered as a separate course (e.g. general science); in the second case, a single syllabus integrates the learning of English with the learning of one or more subjects, as in the Singapore Primary Pilot Project where Maths, Elementary Science and English combine in a closely integrated syllabus.

Within *educational* ESP, then, we distinguish *discipline-based* and *school subject* courses; within *discipline-based* courses we recognize *pre-study* and *in-study* ESP, and within *school subject* ESP are *independent* and *integrated* courses.

The distinctions made thus far provide the teacher of ESP with the primary indications about the kind of learners he will be facing, the content which is going to be appropriate, and the educational level. There remains to be considered a pair of *educational dimensions* which apply to all courses, whether in ESP or in any other branch of language teaching. They are worth mentioning specifically because in ESP they can usually be manipulated, or at least allowed for, much more easily than in conventional ELT. These dimensions are: (i) *proficiency level*, particularly the distinction between *beginners* and *non-beginners*; (ii) *quantity of instruction*, within which the factors of *total number of hours, intensity per week* and *overall duration* are important. Courses can be prepared either for beginners, or for any known point on the scale of proficiency from zero to advanced, and the amount, intensity and duration of the course can sometimes also be re-arranged to meet the needs of the particular learners.

The whole scheme of analysis is summarized in diagram form in Diagram 2: A Taxonomy of ESP Courses.

DIAGRAM 2: A Taxonomy of ESP Courses

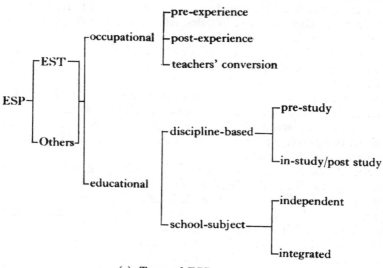

(a) *Types of ESP*

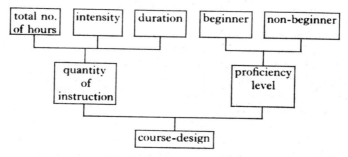

(b) *Pedagogical Dimensions*

A taxonomy of ESP says nothing about two further, vital aspects of the design of any particular course. These aspects are, first, the appropriate *language content*, and second, the *communicative purposes* of the learners.

2. The Language Content

In Chapters 11 and 12 we shall consider in detail the varieties of English; for the present it may be sufficient simply to point out that the English used in each occupation, discipline or school subject that may form the core of an ESP course possesses a recognizable mixture of features of grammar, vocabulary, pronunciation, symbols, styles, etc., which between them characterize the 'register' or variety in question. Not just technical terms, we should notice. Each register consists not of a single element but of a characteristic 'bundle' of features.

'Scientific English', considered in very general terms, possesses no separate, special grammar, no special pronunciation, no special spelling or orthography of words; true, it has some special vocabulary (as well as sharing vocabulary with the whole of the rest of English), and it also employs 'logico-grammatical operators' (*if, although, unless, whenever,* etc), with great precision. But its principal identifying features are statistical, in the sense of being the occurrence, in particular distributions, of bits of English which occur also in non-scientific English, though in different distributions. Thus, 'scientific English' is identified from its frequent use of outstandingly long noun groups (e.g. 'right upper inlet valve spring compression lever'), passive verbs ('steam is raised . . .', *not* 'we raise steam . . .'), abbreviated relatives ('plants capable of self-germination . . .', rather than 'plants *which are* capable of self-germination'), and considerable use of expressions of quantity, together with some special vocabulary and the special symbols used in scientific and technical discourse. (These features are of course only a few of the total range which actually occurs).

So the particular register that is appropriate in a given use of English (such as the use of *given* in this sentence), forms a second part, the language element, which contributes to the design of an ESP course. The third element consists of the *communicative purposes* which the learner seeks to control.

3. Communicative Purposes

It is now common ground among applied linguists that ESP courses should take these into account. Unfortunately, there does not yet exist any final agreement about what the possible range of communicative purposes might be, nor about what to call them. We are at present in the stage where several different writers, faced with the necessity of actually producing materials and wishing to acknowledge as fully as possible the importance of communicative purpose, are each making their own analyses and then comparing them with analyses produced by others. This piecemeal procedure will no doubt eventually throw up major categories recognized by everyone, and these in turn may make possible a further stage of generalization and the formation of hypotheses about communicative categories.

To provide an example, there follows a suggested set of communicative purposes, as they seem to exist in the circumstances of a workshop, factory, laboratory or similar 'technical work-place'. No special justification is attempted for each category, still less for giving each one its particular name. At the same time, discussion with colleagues seems to suggest that these categories largely coincide with what other observers would propose.

'ENGLISH AT WORK': AN ANALYSIS OF COMMUNICATIVE PURPOSES

Introduction

The headings which follow (in the left-hand column) are a summary of communicative purposes as they might be in engineering or technical work, in a factory or similar place of work. The other columns contain examples of spoken and written language to illustrate the categories. In a few places only a list of topics or vocabulary is given, where this seems to be more illuminating than examples of utterances. The scheme as a whole is obviously far from complete, but it illustrates the general principle of analysing communicative purposes, at any rate in one set of conditions.

A distinction is made between three main kinds of communicative purpose: I GENERAL—these are types of communication, spoken and written, which might be found in most engineering or technical places of work, and are not specific to one rather than another. II SOCIAL—these concern relations with workmates, employer, the community at large. III SPECIAL—these are types and topics of communication specific to a particular industry, trade, branch of engineering, etc.

COMMUNICATIVE CATEGORY

EXAMPLES (not exhaustive)

	SPOKEN LANGUAGE	WRITTEN LANGUAGE
1 GENERAL		
A. Instructions		
1. *Receiving and comprehending instructions*	*Oral comprehension* (Imperatives) Run these through. Cut another 25. Bore this out another 5 thou. I want you to do that again. (Oblique Instructions) Better get cracking on that job. It's time these were finished. What are you waiting for?	*Comprehension of written English* Wear hard hat Do not install batteries in these vehicles Machines to be switched off when not attended Re-run whole of batch 697 Today's working pressure: 3.0 Kg/cm²
2. (a) *Giving Instructions*	*Oral Production* Pack 30 in each box. Pass me the micrometer (please). You'll have to replace that drill.	*Written Production* (e.g. on the blackboard, memo sheets, etc.) Next shift: do not use this machine 75 type G required by Tuesday 11.30 p.m. Boiler u/s Use emergency set

(b) *Degrees of authority, formality, politeness, in giving instructions*

(In descending order of formality)
Stop that machine!
Stop that machine, will you?
Stop the machine for a moment, will you?
Do you mind stopping the machine, please?

(Generally, public notices. In descending order of formality)
Employees caught smoking will be dismissed
Smoking forbidden
No smoking, please
If you want to keep your job, don't smoke

3. *Relaying instructions* including reported speech

The foreman says blow it up to 40 p.s.i.
He said we've got to wait.
They want us to stop.

(Notices; written messages)
No drilling today. (Supervisor's orders)
George: telephone Mr. Thomas (signed) Pete
Mr. Thomas wants you to check the inlet temperature

4. *Agreeing; disagreeing*

Yes.
O.K.
Right.
All right.
Yes, I'll do that.
No.
No, I don't think that's right.
No, I can't do that.

(Not normally written.)

5. *Stating Incomprehension*

(I'm sorry) I don't understand.
Please will you explain that again.
Eh? (This is rather abrupt).
I beg your pardon? (This is rather genteel.)

(A large question mark is often written by hand to indicate NOT UNDERSTOOD)

B. Questions

1. *Some Important Types of Questions:*

(a) Verb-first Questions

Is the machine ready?
Must I stop now?
Does this gauge work?

Have you checked the valves?
Are you wearing protective clothing?
Did you switch off the lights?

(b) WH-word Questions

When can I start?
Who is in charge?
Why is the warning light on?
Where is the supervisor?
Which is my place?
What size bolts shall I use?

(Rather rare in public written language.)

(c) HOW + Adjective Questions

How long is the tea-break?
How fast does this motor run?
How many jobs shall I do?

(Rather rare in public written language.)

2. *Querying One's Instructions*	Is this right? Are you sure? Do you mean . . . ? I don't think that's possible. I can't do that, because . . . Would it be better to . . . ?	Always confirm your instructions. After receiving orders by telephone, 　always call back. If in doubt, Ask!
3. *Asking Reasons Why*	Why? What for? What's the reason for that? Who gave the instructions?	(Not normally written)
C. Seeking advice		
1. *Asking for further information*	Please, can you tell me . . . (I'm sorry,) I don't understand. What must I do now?	(Not normally written)
2. *Asking someone to help*	Please will you help me? Please can you show me . . . ? Please can you direct me . . . ? Will you give me a hand, please?	(Not normally written)
3. *Seeking confirmation*	Is this right? Did you say . . . ? Will you repeat that, please? What did you say? I'm sorry, I didn't hear you.	(Not normally written)

D. Stating difficulties or objection

1. *Stating Difficulties*

But . . . .
There isn't enough . . . .
There's too much . . . .
I'm having trouble with this machine.
This isn't working properly.
I haven't got any . . . .

(Not normally written)

2. *Stating Inability or Impossibility*

I can't do that.
I don't know how to do that.
I'm not allowed to do that.
(I'm sorry,) that's impossible.

(Not normally written)

3. *Stating Unwillingness*

I'm not very happy about that.
I don't want to do that.
I'm not going to do that.
I'm not willing to do that.
If I do that, . . .

(Not normally written)

E. Suggesting alternatives

1. *Alternative action*

No, I think . . . instead.
Not X but Y.
It would be better if . . .
I ought to do X, not Y.

(Not normally written)

2. *Alternative personnel*

It's not my job.
It's not my turn.
George should do that.
Why don't you ask Mr. Thomas to do that?

(Not normally written)

F. Measurements and quantities

Dimensions

1. *Comprehending and expressing Quantities*, as appropriate in a given job, within e.g. these dimensions:

— size	— length	— date	— colour
— shape	— breadth	— position	— texture (rough/smooth)
— volume	— thickness	— relative position	— surface
— weight	— number (see below)	— movement	— rate
— temperature	— time	— speed	— curved/linear
	etc.	etc.	etc.
etc.			

2. *Understanding diagrams*

The point of origin . . .
The vertical and horizontal axes . . .
x and y co-ordinates.
The value of . . .
Slope, area, etc.

Diagrams; values expressed in terms of co-ordinates; simple algebraic expressions.

3. *Understanding and verbalizing numbers; also common symbols*

twelve point three-two	12.32
five and three-sixteenths	$5\frac{3}{16}$
twenty-one thou	$\frac{21}{1000}$
four plus seven; four times seven; four divided by seven; four minus seven; four over seven	$4+7; 4\times7; 4\div7; 4-7; \frac{4}{7}$
x squared	x^2
the square root of seventeen point seven	$\sqrt{17.7}$
two pi r	$2\pi r$
eleven thirty-seven	(time) 11.37
the seventh of June	June 7th
nineteen-eighty	1980
three metres	3 metres
eighty-three centimetres	83 cm
eleven millimetres	11 mm
etc.	etc.

G. Dangers and emergencies; signals; safety rules

1. *Public instructions, notices and tannoy (public address) announcements*

Attention please. This is an emergency. There is an outbreak of fire in the paint shop. All parts of the building are to be evacuated at once. There's no need for panic. Follow your fire-drill procedures.	Fire In case of fire, use the alarm Fire-parties assemble at their stations Now Evacuate the building in an orderly manner Don't panic

N.O.—8

2. *Types of danger*	Fire; electrical short-circuit; explosion; burst pipe; steam; escape of gas; building collapse; crash; collision; kidnap; flames; sparks; fumes; smoke; etc.	(Not usually written)
3. *Warning others of danger*	Fire! Look out! Get out quickly! Stand back! Keep clear! Stop! Go back!	Fire warning: wailing siren
4. *Sound signals*	Whistle; siren; hooter; buzzer; bleeper; bell; gong; continuous; intermittent; wailing.	
5. *Visual signals*	Lights; colours; flashing; lights on/out; lights on/off; etc.	(Not usually written)

H. Injury, health

1. *Types of hazard*	Electrocution; crushing; falling from a height; drowning; suffocation; smothering; choking; burning; scalding; deafening; blinding; slipping; exposure; freezing; radiation.	Wear hard hat Hard hat area Danger—high voltage Beware of fumes Radiation hazard Storm warning

2. *Personal conditions*

Pain; fainting; unconsciousness; coma: fever; sickness; nausea; diarrhoea.

3. *Types of injury*

Broken; fractured; crushed; cut; burned; scalded; bleeding; bruised.

4. *Casualty states*

Dead; injured; hurt; missing; degrees of injury—slight, severe, etc.

5. *Parts of the body*

'Everyday' vocabulary—i.e. not technical medical terms.

6. *Emergency services and personnel*

Fire service; fire brigade; fireman; doctor; nurse; ambulance; ambulance man; first aid; police; policeman; etc.

II SOCIAL COMMUNICATION

A. Face-to-face conversation, and related written communication

1. *Personal identity: name, age, origin, job, family, home details*

I'm George Nikas.
My name is George Nikas.
I'm 29 (years old).
I come from . . .
I'm an electrical fitter.
I'm married, and I've got two sons and one daughter.
I'm Helena Nikas. I'm 19.
I'm not married, but I'm engaged.

Bus from Highfield Estate leaves from here
M/F (Delete where not applicable).
Fill in name, age, occupation and permanent address. Sign on dotted line.
Marital status: married/single

2. Greetings and polite expressions; chat about sport, radio, T.V., pop music, politics; 'phatic communion', etc. (Depends largely on individual interests.)	Hello. Good morning, etc. Are you a Spurs fan? What won the 2.30? Did you see Kojak last night? Why weren't you at the pub last night? Are you going to vote? Turned out nice. This weather makes you sick.	(Not written)
3. Washroom details	Where's the washroom? Where's the toilet? Where's the loo? etc. I'm going to wash my hands.	Men Women Gents Ladies W.C. Washroom Restroom
4. Working hours, breaks, meal-times	I'm on the early shift. How much overtime do you work? How long is this break? What time is the lunch break?	Shift Hours: 6.30–2.30 2.30–10.30 10.30–6.30 Punch your card before entering Second sitting for lunch: 1.15
5. Discussion of management, workers, unions	Who's the supervisor? What are the bosses like? That's the shop steward. The works manager is showing round some visitors.	Supervisor's office Union cards to be shown Wear I.D. at all times

6. *Pay, conditions, documents*

My immediate boss is the Deputy Accountant.
There are 17 men in this section.
Which union do you belong to?

I'm on the hourly rate.
When do we get a rise?
They pay us on the last Friday of the month.
We ought to get protective clothing.
They took too much off my pay last week.
I'm on the wrong tax code.
They forgot to stamp my N.I. card.
This pay-slip is wrong.

Collect pay-packets here
Gross pay £47.50
Deductions:
P.A.Y.E. £9.90
N.I. 4.80
Union .50
Total deduction £15.20
Net Pay: £32.30

7. *Discussion of cultural differences*
(Food; clothing; marriage and family; etc.)

(According to local needs)

B. **Receiving and making telephone calls**

1. *Speaking phone numbers*

Six-two-nine, eight-four-nine-four
STD code, oh-three-one
Extension two-three-one-three

629-8494
STD: 031
Ext. 2313

2. *Telephone techniques*

Dialling tone; ringing tone; number engaged; number out of order; etc.

Public Telephone
STD codes
Telephone Directory
Directory Enquiries

George Nikas here.
Can I speak to Mr. Thomas, please?
Is that Mr. Thomas?
Will you ask him to come to the phone, please?
Please ask him to ring me back.

III SPECIAL COMMUNICATIVE PURPOSES
(N.B.: These will depend on the specific occupation.)

A. **Operating Safety Rules**

B. **Protective Clothing and Equipment**

C. **Particular hazards**

D. **Tools, Equipment, Instruments, Materials**

E. **Individual Tasks; Separate Stages/Processes**

F. **Special Register Features** (e.g. Sailors speak of a ship as *she*, not *it*; special colloquialisms used among members of a particular occupation, etc.)

The preceding tabulation is intended to show one way in which the idea of communicative purpose may be applied in the preparation of ESP teaching materials. It illustrates why very much more has to be specified than a simple list of vocabulary items and a list of 'structures' and grammatical teaching points; it shows at the same time that the language being selected is directly relevant to the communicative needs of the learner; and it also illustrates the chief problem generated by this approach, namely that when the moment arrives to actually teach the total collection of relevant language, one finds that it covers a very wide range of complexity. It is relatively simple to teach comprehension of the written messages WEAR HARD HAT or DANGER: HIGH VOLTAGE. But it is much more difficult to teach a spoken command of English that embraces both *Don't touch that machine!* and also *I think you'd better check with the supervisor.*

Of course, the particular tabulation set out earlier in this chapter is only one writer's response to one set of learners' circumstances, and to the communicative purposes which that writer perceives, perhaps incorrectly, to be the needs of those learners. Learners are not aware of their own language requirements, and external observers (e.g. textbook writers and applied linguists) have only experience and intuition to guide them. In consequence, different observers arrive at different analyses of the situation; indeed, one of the difficulties facing teachers on first entering the field of ESP is that many different writers have each proposed their own list of headings, often apparently overlapping with each other. Even more confusing, different writers tend to use, often without adequate definition, one or more of the labels *notional, functional* or *communicative.*

What do these terms mean? All three relate to generalizations, but of different kinds. *Notions* are generalizations about the nature of the universe—time, space, location, shape, moral and emotional attitudes, for example—and they are important for language teaching because they provide the course designer with a fairly small number of labels for referring to a vast array of concepts. *Functions* are generalizations about what language does—for example *the inter-personal function of language* is the role played by language in making, operating, describing, etc. the relationships between people. *Communicative categories* are generalizations about the ways in which people address each other, communicate with each other, influence each other, through language— for example by explanation, contradiction, giving information, asking questions, apologizing, stating objections, etc.

The development of special-purpose language teaching has both encouraged and been helped by the simultaneous drive to elaborate concepts of notions, functions and communicative purposes. These ideas enable the course designer to be much more precise in fitting his teaching materials to the needs of the learners, and this is an advantage, since it seems that there is a direct relation between how relevant a learner perceives his course to be and how well he learns. But at the same time, greater precision in identifying the learner's true needs brings the consequence of greater complexity in the teaching matter that has to be organized into a coherent course. ESP, when developed to the limit of the art, brings improved learning but requires teachers of more advanced experience and training. It is emphatically not a quick and easy option for below-average teachers.

9 The learning and teaching of reading

For more than a quarter of a century, language teachers have been dominated by the idea that speech is the primary form of language, writing is secondary. Acting on this idea, language teaching has tended to concentrate on teaching the ability to understand speech and to speak comprehensibly; reading and writing have been given less attention.

This emphasis was no doubt useful as a counterbalance to the idea, inherent in grammar-translation methods of teaching, that 'language' means written language. But the pendulum may have swung too far in the direction of speech, and many teachers are now seeking to increase the effort applied to learning and teaching a command of the written language, and especially to the learning and teaching of reading.

In this chapter we shall consider three points relating to reading. First, the fact that reading is exceedingly complex: we shall attempt a summary of the elements involved in reading. Second, the fact that those who are learning to read can be distinguished according to the stage of proficiency they have reached; relating these distinctions to the activities of reading, we shall offer working definitions for the conventional labels 'beginner', 'intermediate' and 'advanced'. Third, we shall look at some of the practical consequences for teaching brought about by the sequence of changes which take place in learning as the learner's proficiency in reading develops through these stages.

1. Reading is a Complex Activity

What *is* reading? Reading consists of making out the meaning of written language. (It is worth remembering that large numbers of languages do not exist in written form, and that reading and writing are far from universal.) An analysis of reading must embody an analysis of writing.

1. *The nature of reading*
   (i) *Reading is visual.* Reading is carried out through the sense of sight, which carries some limitations but many advantages. Effective reading requires the training of the muscles of the eye to perform a number of tasks: to change focus as necessary; to

seek a brief, large-scale, general view of the text; to find a starting-point; to change focus and scale so as to identify the language at the starting-point; and then to follow along the text altering direction as needed, and proceeding at a speed which meets the understanding rate of the learner's brain.

(ii) *Reading is organized and systematic.* Written language possesses beginnings and endings. (If this seems trivial, consider a text in an unfamiliar language with a very different writing system: where does the text begin? In which direction should the eye travel? Where is the end?) It contains many internal breaks and divisions—spaces between letters or characters; bigger spaces between words; bigger ones still between sentences; spaces between lines; paragraph divisions; chapter divisions; the conventions of punctuation; etc. It selects, separately for each language, a set of visual symbols—letters or characters, together with diacritics, upper-case/lower-case distinctions, different styles of representation of the same shape (roman, italic, Gothic, printed or handwritten, etc.)—and it arranges these symbols in sequences or strings of varying length. The strings are always arranged in a linear sequence, but the lines may be either horizontal or vertical, and if horizontal they may run either from left to right as in English or right to left as in Arabic. Sometimes the symbols may be arranged on the page in a way which evokes artistic or aesthetic meaning, as in poetry, or as in the 'Mouse's Tale' in *Alice in Wonderland*. The reader has to learn to be familiar with all these conventions of shape, sequence, arrangement, visual effect.

(iii) *Reading is arbitrary and abstract, but meaningful.* With some rare and partial exceptions (e.g. Egyptian hieroglyphics; some characters in Chinese) the shapes of the symbols used in written language are arbitrary—they are unrelated to the real-life forms of whatever it is they refer to, just as the shape of the figure 5 is unrelated to the properties of the number 5. Letters, words, sentences and longer stretches of text relate to meanings of several kinds, and these relations are specific to each particular language. At the same time, written language always embodies visual clues to information, of three kinds: of a *grammatical* kind, a *lexical* kind, and a *semantic* kind; and in most writing systems the written language is a direct transform of the spoken language. Writing represents speech, not vice versa.

(iv) *Related to a particular language and society.* But writing is not solely a mechanical process. It has great social and cultural importance. It can become the embodiment of the history, achievement, customs, literature, values, beliefs, of a whole people, because it can build up and fix over a long period the reflection of a society's organized thought. However, the transmission of culture and ideas is only one of the functions which writing performs: it is to these functions that we should now turn.

2. *The functions of written language:* to convey meaning. Written language conveys meanings of at least six kinds:

(i) *Iconic.* By exercising choice among different shapes and styles of writing—the use of italics, or capitals, or decorated initials, etc. —a particular range of meanings can be employed. In written Japanese, for example, this range of possibilities includes the art-form of calligraphy. On a different scale, copperplate and italic have their significance in handwriting, as do different typefaces in printing.

(ii) *Linguistic.* This is the function of written language which is most frequently considered, often to the exclusion of all others. Writing embodies and conveys the forms of the language, in a grammatical, lexical, semantic, stylistic, even phonological sense. This is the function of writing which embodies a description of the language in all its forms and all its diversity.

(iii) *Logical.* A function of language that is often ignored but which is perhaps especially important as a function of written language, at least in intellectually dense texts, is the function of indicating logical relations. Words such as *and, but, or, unless, if, although, whenever,* can convey strictly logical meanings of a precise, universal kind. Indeed, logical relations, implications and presuppositions are more effectively—and more often—conveyed in writing than in speech. Language is not logic: logic stands outside language. But logical relations are expressed or implied in language. Learning to read includes becoming familiar, often for the first time, with a small number of logical features.

(iv) *Informational.* Written texts are generally 'about' something. They contain meanings that inform the reader, that provide him with knowledge or understanding. Some kinds of written texts perform this function more fully than others. This is the 'content' aspect of written language, and it is what teachers usually refer to when they speak of 'reading comprehension'.

(v) *Rhetorical.* A piece of writing may narrate, describe, explain, exhort, command, threaten, amuse, deceive—the communicative purposes of the writer towards the reader are conveyed through this rhetorical function of written language.

(vi) *Implicational.* Even more elusive than the rhetoric of a piece of written language is its ability to convey implications and inferences, which are in part a compound of the logic, the information and the rhetoric, and yet which can be deliberately inserted in a passage, or alternatively can be elucidated by the reader without the writer having been consciously aware of them. This implicational function also includes the expression of relations between the writer and those he was addressing, about the situation which led to the communication taking place; and so forth.

These six functions of written language only operate fully when the reader is affected by them in the way intended by the writer; so they can be regarded not only as functions of written language but also as functions of *reading*. Now we must ask, by what processes does the reader fulfil these functions?

3. *The processes carried out by the reader*

It seems necessary to distinguish two different kinds of process. The first, which I shall call *deciphering*, is visual in nature; the second, which I shall call *decoding*, is semantic in nature.

(a) *Deciphering:* this is a form of pattern-recognition. The reader learns to distinguish writing from other kinds of pattern, learns the letter-shapes, becomes accustomed to the direction of writing, finds beginnings and ends, identifies words, sentences, paragraphs, learns to adjust the rate of eye-scan to the rate of comprehension, and also learns how to refer back—or forward—to resolve ambiguity or doubt.

(b) *Decoding:* this is part of the total process of comprehension. It entails linking the flow of deciphered information to the reader's knowledge of the language—its grammar, vocabulary, semantics, pronunciation—and of the culture. The reader has to bring together *vision*, *hearing*, *memory* and *imagination*, in order to discover the meaning, interpret it, and perhaps put it into action; and finally the language he has read is assimilated into his total experience, thereby affecting in some degree all his subsequent reading.

2. Stages of Proficiency

The purpose of giving this detailed description of what is involved in reading has been to show that a large number of activities, of very different kinds, have to be learned. But not all the activities are, or can be, learned at the same time; some necessarily precede others—for example, pattern recognition (deciphering) necessarily precedes comprehension (decoding). In the early stages, the learner is trying to answer questions like 'What letter is that?' 'What's that word?' 'Is this word the same as that word?' 'Why is that letter shaped differently?' 'Does this capital letter tell me something special?' 'How does this sentence hang together?' Only later does he move on to answer questions like 'What does this sentence mean?' 'How does the meaning of this sentence modify or confirm my understanding of what the past three paragraphs have been about?' 'Is this statement (which I understand) true?' 'What is the writer trying to persuade me to believe?'

It is common experience among teachers that changes in the activities of learners occur as they learn to read, and that these changes occur in a standard sequence. At the very outset—stage (a)—even pattern recognition is difficult; probably no comprehension takes place at all for a while, except that which is deliberately fed to the learner, piecemeal, by the teacher. Later—stage (b)—pattern recognition and deciphering become easy, and the growth of comprehension begins, though this may be slow and patchy. Eventually—stage (c)—deciphering may be done without conscious effort, and comprehension will become faster, more fluent, with fewer obstacles and impediments.

The three stages (a), (b) and (c), chosen for illustrating progress in learning to read, remind us of similar states in the general, overall progress of foreign language learning, to which the labels 'beginner', 'intermediate' and 'advanced' are generally applied, though those labels are usually used loosely, intuitively, subjectively, and without being expressed verbally. We may look briefly at what is usually meant by each of these labels in general terms, and then compare those descriptions with their equivalents in reading progress.

Beginner. The beginner is completely or largely uncomprehending and incomprehensible. He or she is unable to understand the foreign language when it is spoken or written, and cannot speak or write it— except as he is led to do so, item by item, by the teacher. (The teacher' here may include the course-book and other materials.) So the beginner is heavily dependent on the teacher, and the teacher has total responsibility for helping the beginner to achieve enough success to be encouraged to go on learning. The beginner starts to become an intermediate student when he achieves success by his own efforts—when he understands at least the gist of a sentence, or when he produces a sentence or utterance which is comprehended, without being led to this achievement solely by the teacher's instruction. Being a beginner is very unsatisfactory: the beginner's discovery of even limited success is often very exciting.

Intermediate Learner. The intermediate stage of learning a language is the longest, and it shades from the beginning and into the advanced stages rather imperceptibly. During this intermediate stage the learner at first becomes able to get and to produce the gist of the language; then he increases his degree of *independence* of explicit guidance, the *rate* at which he can handle the foreign language, his *accuracy* in doing so, and the *continuity* of his effort—that is, he is reducing hesitations, errors,

circumlocutions, translation time, etc.—and his *coverage* of the language
—vocabulary, grammatical rules, pronunciation, acceptance of stylistic
variation, and so forth. The task of the teacher is to help the intermediate learner maintain his sense of achievement; to provide him with
enough quantity of the foreign language to satisfy his learning pace, but
not so much that he is swamped by unfamiliarity or checked by too
high a rate of errors; to guard against the emergence of habitual errors
having grammatical importance; to balance the necessary quantity of
experience with sufficient practice, consolidation and correction; and to
lead him towards the 'take-off velocity' of the advanced learner.

Advanced Learner. The learner becomes 'advanced' as he becomes able,
occasionally at first, but with increasing frequency and for lengthening
stretches of the foreign language, to dispense with the mediation of his
own language. It is too facile to say simply that he 'ceases to mentally
translate'; it is too imprecise to say that he 'begins to think in the
foreign language'. Nevertheless, both these inexact notions seem to
relate to what teachers observe, which is that the learners have recourse
less and less frequently to their own language, and that they use the
foreign language more and more at the rate, with the precision and in
the manner, of the native speaker. The teacher's task now is to find and
supply language material that is sufficiently interesting to the learner,
and that does not interrupt the momentum of his learning; to help him
to identify the gaps in his language experience and ensure that they are
filled; to lead the learner towards the limits of his personal language-
learning ability.

3. Practical Consequences in the Teaching of Reading

Putting the teaching of reading into these perspectives—that is to say,
first into the perspective of the nature of reading, and second into the
perspective of stages of language learning—it becomes possible to see
justification for much of what is already done, but also to suggest what
might be done that is only rarely encountered.

Teaching the beginning reader

What needs to be done, and how best to achieve it, depends greatly on
whether the learner has ever learned to read in any other language, and
if so, how that language compares, especially in its writing system, with
English, or any other language being taught. Even so, all learners begin
by facing the task of pattern recognition, so that there is an inescapable
phase for all learners during which they must learn to recognize and
identify the written letters: distinguishing small and capital letters,
learning both print and handwriting, mastering the system of punctuation, and becoming familiar with the direction of flow of the written

language. In the beginning stage, also, the learner has to establish the relations between speech and writing, so that henceforth he 'knows' the language in both its manifestations, spoken and written, and can switch between the sense-modalities of vision and hearing without conscious effort. This is where the learner encounters the spelling system of the language, learning it first through the most frequent correspondences between letters and sounds, and gradually extending his command to less frequent correspondences, irregular words (e.g. -ough words in English), isolated peculiarities. Throughout this period, learning to read may be assisted by learning to write, so that receptive and productive faculties, and several different sets of muscles, reinforce each other and contribute to the learning effect. Thus the learner learns to control the *iconic* character of language while at the same time he is learning the rudiments of its *linguistic* character. Techniques and materials for teaching reading at this stage are, on the whole, widely known and available.

Teaching the intermediate reader

The principal technique in current use for teaching reading at the intermediate stage is that of supplementary, graded readers. It is generally accepted that the achievement of fluency and of a wider coverage of the language are desirable aims, and most teachers strive to obtain a large quantity of reading matter, often distinguishing between *intensive* and *extensive* reading. Two sources of difficulty exist: first, it is extremely difficult, in practice, for the teacher to meet the needs of each individual learner at the various different times that individuals actually become intermediate learners. Classwork presupposes that all learners progress from one stage to another at the same moment, which is not true. To try and get over this problem there is currently a wave of interest in *individualization*, that is, in providing within a common framework the opportunity for each individual learner to learn at least partly at his own rate. In reading, this is promoted by the provision of numbers of separate materials—lots of small books, or leaflets, or cards—which become longer and more complex. (Reading kits are a case in point.) This trend is certain to increase.

The second difficulty is that the grading of reading materials has often proved inadequate, in two senses: (a) by being self-defeating, so that 'simplified' texts have frequently been 'simplified' out of all sensible meaning; and (b) by the fact that many learners find vocabulary graded materials unappetizing: not that they *can't* learn from them, but that they *won't*. What is now being realized is that the grading of reading materials, and above all the *choice* of texts, must reflect not only characteristics of the *language* (vocabulary, grammar, etc.) but also characteristics of the *learner*. What he is *willing* to read and what he is *interested* to read are products of his sex, age-group, level of education, degree of intellectuality, personal interests, etc. Reading materials are increasingly being designed to fit both the learner's level of proficiency in English and his reading interests. In so doing, they are providing the learner with the means of developing further command of the *linguistic* meanings of writing, enabling him to grasp *informational* and *logical* meanings, and perhaps starting him on the understanding of *rhetorical* and *implicational* meanings.

Teaching the advanced reader

In some senses, the task of teaching reading at the advanced stage is no longer a language task, but is a contribution to the general education and intellectual development of the learner, at whatever point he may be, since in his reading he is now dealing with *ideas*, as well as *information*, conveyed in written language. That is perhaps why rather little satisfactory advanced reading material is available.

There is a difficulty here: the range of possible materials is extremely wide, as also is the range of interests of the learners themselves. For one learner it is satisfactory to use poetry and other works of literature, at least if these are suitably annotated and prepared. For another learner, literature is thoroughly unwelcome: what *he* wants is 'general interest' reading—magazines, newspapers, etc. Others want non-fiction or specific topics in science and technology. (This may account for some of the success of special-purpose language teaching: at the advanced level these learners receive materials which are of direct relevance and interest to them.) In general, there are not yet enough advanced reading materials, over a sufficiently wide range of interests and levels of educational and intellectual development. Materials are required that lead the learner to a surer grasp of *logical, rhetorical* and *implicational* meanings.

Conclusion

To sum up, reading is a complex activity, and the learner progresses through different segments of it as he advances in proficiency. This progression is broadly parallel to the general stages of learning usually called *beginning, intermediate* and *advanced*. Techniques and materials for teaching beginners are well known and reasonably satisfactory; at the later stages there is a need for the development and provision of a great deal of fresh material.

Part Four

The Language We Teach

10 Varieties of English: the description of diversity

One of the requirements which bears upon every language teacher is that he or she should be 'familiar' with the language he teaches. This 'familiarity' entails above all possessing a command of the language adequate for his teaching purposes (see Chapter 6, p. 74); but it also entails knowing a certain amount *about* the language. The first of these requirements might be called *performative skill* in the language, while the second is *cognitive knowledge* about the language.

In this chapter and the next we shall concentrate on the second of these requirements, and particularly on one kind of knowledge about English which has become available to the EFL teacher in recent years and which is beginning to affect the nature of teaching courses and materials. We are referring to knowledge of the great diversity of English, and hence knowledge of the principal dimensions which determine *the varieties of English*, to the extent that these varieties are relevant to the learning and teaching of English as a foreign or second language.

In contrast with the situation of twenty years ago, most teachers of English are nowadays aware that English is not a single, homogeneous language. They are aware, too, of the idea of 'varieties' of English, and they probably know the term 'register'—a variety related to a particular use of the language, a particular subject or occupation—though teaching materials which can help the teacher to make use of the idea of register are still rather rare. Teachers wishing to extend their familiarity with English by understanding better its diversity and the range and function of the varieties of English do not need to be persuaded that varieties exist. Nor is there any longer a shortage of published work on the subject. The difficulty is rather that much of the published work is inaccessible to teachers (because it has been published in journals outside the range of professional journals commonly seen by teachers of English) and that when they do come across articles or books on the subject there appear to be a number of different approaches to the subject, some of them more obviously relevant than others.

Two principal ways of studying varieties of language seem to have emerged: a *sociolinguistic* approach, and a *description of English* approach.

The main purpose of this chapter is to outline these approaches. The following chapter then provides a formulation designed to be particularly useful to the teacher of English as a foreign language.

I

A Sociolinguistic Approach to Varieties

The teacher of English trying to keep abreast of developments in linguistics faces a difficulty: linguistics has developed and extended in a rather short period of time until it now embraces a number of different types of discipline, some of which are more concerned with formal, mathematical or philosophical studies, some with psychological aspects of language, some with language in relation to society. As far as the phenomenon of variation within languages is concerned, both formal and psychological linguistics can either ignore the existence of such varieties or at most can touch on them superficially, since within these disciplines language is studied in an 'idealized' form and with no requirement to provide techniques for the description of spoken or written texts. In sociolinguistics, by contrast, this very diversity of language makes up a major part of the complex phenomena which linguists interested in society and sociologists interested in language seek to understand, explain and describe.

Sociolinguistics begins from the assumption or observation that whenever language happens—that is, whenever someone speaks or listens or reads or writes—it happens within a social context. This means that there is a particular occasion for the piece of language in question to occur, the person or people involved have particular identities both as individuals and as members of their society at large, and the 'language event' has specific intention and function. All this may at first sight seem to be stating the obvious, and in a rather complicated way. But the study of diversity in language is the study of the reasons why people say and write precisely what they do say and write, instead of using any of the other possible ways of writing or saying 'the same thing', and it turns out that the reasons are highly complex and therefore require a complex framework of categories to explain them.

In a famous article, Dell Hymes (1972) summarized the '. . . kinds of components co-present in a communicative event'. 'Briefly put, (1, 2) the various kinds of participants in communicative events—senders and receivers, addressors and addressees, interpreters and spokesmen, and the like; (3) the various available channels, and their modes of use, speaking, writing, printing, drumming, blowing, whistling, singing, face and body motion as visually received, smelling, tasting and tactile sensation; (4) the various codes shared by various participants, linguistic, paralinguistic, kinesic, musical and other; (5) the settings (including other communication) in which communication is permitted, enjoined, encouraged, abridged; (6) the forms of messages, and their genres, ranging verbally from single-morpheme sentences to the patterns and diacritics of sonnets, sermons, salesmen's pitches and any other organized routines and styles; (7) the topics and comments that a message may be about; (8) the events themselves, their kinds and characters as wholes—all these must be identified in an adequate ethnographic way.'

Sociolinguistics is also interested in the way in which every human being, through a lifelong and continual process of verbal interaction with others, discovers himself, learns who he is and what relation he has to other people, and maintains or changes this personal and social identity. This process begins in the child's home, continues through his schooling, then enters a further phase in adulthood. Throughout his life he will be involved—passively, actively, interactively—in communication through language, and he learns at an early age that 'communicative competence' requires him to master the proper selection and accurate use of the many alternative variations of language that are open to him.

Language, then, does not relate solely to the social context which as it were surrounds the speaker at the moment of utterance, it also relates to the individual's own concept of himself, his relationship to others, and so eventually to his total view of the universe. Human beings are what they are *because of language*, which permits and demands interaction between people, as well as providing channels for information, description, persuasion, etc. Consequently, sociolinguists find it essential to take into account the individual's acquisition of language, the role and function of language in his education, even the 'sociology of his knowledge' and his construction of a model of reality.

From the point of view of this chapter, the relevance of the subtle and complex distinctions which sociolinguistics is becoming able to understand, is that in most cases they are conveyed by subtle and complex choices of syntax and grammar, vocabulary, tempo, rhythm, tone of voice, accompanying gesture, eye-contact, and so forth. Such choices, continually being made by every individual and understood by those he is communicating with, through the use of one variety or sub-variety of language rather than another, maintaining and sustaining the fabric and intercourse of society—these constitute the basic evidence on which rests the science of sociolinguistics. And within sociolinguistics the focus of interest may be upon special areas such as: (i) the individual as a member of society; (ii) society and the languages used by its members; (iii) language and interactions between individuals; (iv) linguistic interactions between different societies; (v) development of a unified theory of sociolinguistics.

Varieties of English, from a sociolinguistic standpoint, thus become a manifestation, of (i) the geographical and social origins of the individual, and of the extent to which his schooling reinforces or loosens the characteristics of social class (in dialect, accent, command of elaborated or restricted 'codes', etc.); of (ii) attitudes towards 'standard' and 'non-standard' usage, of the selection (e.g. in Malaysia or Tanzania, or Quebec, or Belgium, etc.) of particular languages for precedence in a multilingual society, and of attitudes towards the learning and teaching of foreign languages; of (iii) the diverse and subtle yet crucially important ways in which people organize their language when communicating with each other (e.g. as when a teacher says 'Right! Now . . .' he is at once understood to be proposing a break in the thread of meaning, a change of subject, a fresh activity, a course of action in which others will be involved, etc.) of (iv) the development of pidgins and creoles (pp. 140–1), the emergence of new languages, the processes of borrowing and other influences from one language to another; and of (v) the integration of all these phenomena into a single theoretical framework, compatible with theoretical standpoints in sociology, anthropology and other branches of the science of man.

The foregoing sketch of a sociolinguistic approach to the study of varieties in language is intended as both an encouragement to the teacher and a warning: an encouragement, in the sense that the teacher should feel that sociolinguistics concerns itself with understanding and explaining some aspects of language that are central in the teacher's professional life; and a warning in the sense that the aims, techniques and theories of the science of sociolinguistics are not those of the art of language teaching, and must not be approached in the expectation that they will be self-evident, or intellectually simple.

II

A 'Description of English' Approach to Varieties

Much closer to the needs of the classroom teacher of English is the work of those who concern themselves with the description of English, in the long tradition of (among others) Sweet, Jespersen, Palmer.

Here we should beware of a play on words. *Linguistic* is a perfectly acceptable adjective from *language*; but the same word, *linguistic*, is also a perfectly acceptable adjective from *linguistics*. In the early days of the development of linguistics as an independent discipline the confusion of terms was a minor one, partly because many of those engaged in linguistics were also eminent in the field of English studies, and partly because linguistics passed through a stage in which its main thrust was descriptive. As linguistics developed, however, it began to range more widely than the description of any single language, to concern itself with more than description, and even to re-assess the part that the description of a language could and should play within linguistics as a whole.

While linguistics was thus amending its philosophical bases, the analysis and description of English continued to be the major concern of another branch of academic study, and those engaged in it found quite frequently that linguistics could provide for them new insights, new techniques, new illumination upon the nature of the English language. Nevertheless, the aim and focus of the description of English remained distinct and separate from the aims of linguistics.

The reasons for dwelling upon this play upon the word *linguistic* and for emphasizing the distinct though related nature of English studies and linguistics are first, to remind ourselves of the tradition of descriptive work on English; second, to recall that although linguistics is an important discipline it is by no means necessary that teachers of English should regard linguistics as in some way dominating ELT; and finally, to introduce a brief outline of two contributions to work on varieties, which combine insights derived from both linguistics and the 'description of English' tradition.

One direction in the descriptive study of varieties was taken by M. Gregory, *Aspects of Varieties Differentiation*. His starting point was broadly the same as that which will inform the next chapter (i.e. a language teaching approach); it was based on work done by J. C. Catford, *A Linguistic Theory of Translation*, and by M. A. K. Halliday, A. McIntosh and P. Strevens, *The Linguistic Sciences and Language Teaching*. But Gregory went further in some parts of his analysis than others have done before or since, particularly in his analysis of what he calls 'user's medium relationship'—roughly, different kinds of speaking and writing—and he illuminated his position by the use of three diagrams, which are reproduced here with the author's permission.

Gregory's first group of categories he refers to as *dialectal varieties*, 'the linguistic reflection of reasonably permanent characteristics of the USER in language situations'. The general word 'dialect' is here given a range of fine distinctions in meaning. (See Diagram 3)

The term *dialectal variety* refers to the features of a person's speech or of what he has written which enable us to identify that person rather than another (individuality: I can recognize Mr X or Miss Y); to recognize the English of one historical period rather than another (temporal provenance: that text reads like Elizabethan English or Victorian English); to judge where a speaker or writer comes from (geographical provenance: he is a Yorkshireman, she is West Indian); to form an opinion about class origins (social provenance: upper class, middle class, working class); to decide whether the English we hear or read is 'standard' or 'non-standard' (range of intelligibility: Standard English, Non-standard English).

DIAGRAM 3
suggested categories of dialectal variety differentiation

situational categories	contextual categories	examples of English varieties (*descriptive contextual categories*)	DIALECTAL VARIETIES: the linguistic reflection of reasonably permanent characteristics of the USER in language situations
individuality	idiolect	Mr. X's English, Miss Y's English	
temporal provenance	temporal dialect	Old English, Modern English	
geographical provenance	geographical dialect	British English, American English	
social provenance	social dialect	Upper Class English, Middle Class English	
range of intelligibility	standard/non-standard dialect	Standard English, Non-Standard English	

user's

DIAGRAM 4

suggested categories of diatypic variety differentiation

situational categories	*contextual categories*	*examples of English varieties (descriptive contextual categories)*	DIATYPIC VARIETIES: the linguistic reflection of recurrent characteristics of user's USE of language in situations
purposive role	field of discourse	Technical English, Non-Technical English	
medium relationship	mode of discourse	Spoken English, Written English	
addressee relationship	tenor of discourse		
user's (a) personal	personal tenor	Formal English, Informal English	
(b) functional	functional tenor	Didactic English, Non-Didactic English	

Gregory has suggested categories of *diatypic varieties*, 'the linguistic reflection of recurrent characteristics of the user's USE of language in situations'. These categories include distinctions such as *technical/non-technical* and *formal/informal*. (See Diagram 4)

Gregory uses the term *diatypic varieties* to refer to subject matter (purposive role: a field of science, or swapping jokes in a social situation); the choice of either speech or writing (mode of discourse); and the relationship between the speaker or writer and those to whom one speaks or for whom one is writing (addressee relationship: formal or informal language, the use of language appropriate to e.g. lecturing, writing a diary, giving a pep talk to a flagging football team, etc.).

Also proposed are a number of categories of *user's medium relationship*, in which Gregory is able to allow for the distinctions we all use and recognize between, e.g. *conversing* and *monologuing*, *writing to be spoken as if not written* and *writing not necessarily to be spoken*, and several others. (See Diagram 5)

This is the only analysis of English, as far as I know, which takes account of differences such as those between 'reciting', where the speaker has learned a text by heart and speaks it to an audience who know that this is the case, and 'the speaking of what is written', for instance in speaking a radio news bulletin; between written texts 'to be spoken as if not written', such as the words of plays and films and some political speeches, and written texts 'not necessarily to be spoken', such as dialogue in novels.

Gregory's distinctions are not easy to apply in practical ways, but they repay study because they bring to the surface some subtle differences which all native speakers of English operate without conscious thought yet which constitute a set of considerable barriers for the foreign learner.

The second illustration of recent work on the description of varieties is taken from the works which have emerged as a result of the massive Survey of English Usage, conducted by Professor Randolph Quirk. *A Grammar of Contemporary English* (R. Quirk, S. Greenbaum, G. Leech and J. Svartvik) stands at the apex of the descriptive tradition we noted earlier, and is certain to be the most comprehensive and illuminating reference work on contemporary English for the next half-century.

It is significant that in the *Grammar of Contemporary English*, Quirk and his collaborators devote twenty pages of Chapter One to 'Varieties of English and classes of varieties'. They postulate a Common Core of English, containing the following classes of variety: *region; education and social standing; subject matter; medium; attitude; interference*. Each class of variety contains within it a number of varieties, and '. . . we need to see a common core or nucleus that we call "English"

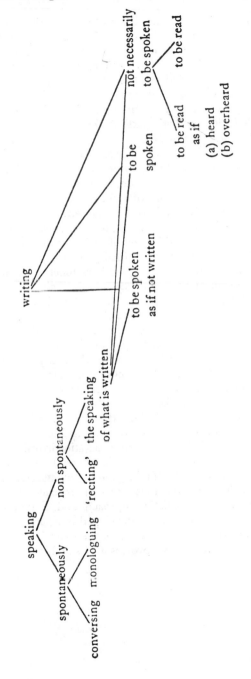

DIAGRAM 5
suggested distinctions along the dimension of situation variation
categorised as user's medium relationship

being realized only in the different actual varieties of the language that we hear or read' (R. Quirk et al., *A Grammar of Contemporary English*).

Quirk's classes of variety are easy to grasp. *Regional variation* relates to *dialects* and is realized in differences of grammar, vocabulary, and especially pronunciation. *Variation by education and social standing* introduces a discussion of 'Standard English' and of the relatively small differences which can be discerned in various national standards of English, including British and American English. *Varieties according to subject matter* are briefly discussed in relation to both vocabulary and grammar. *Varieties according to medium* (i.e. in speech or in writing) are touched on, and the difficulty of indicating in writing the devices used in speech (e.g. stress, rhythm, intonation, tempo) are outlined. *Attitudinal varieties* are more difficult to explain and describe; a potential five-term set of distinctions is suggested:

(rigid)—FORMAL—normal—INFORMAL—(familiar)

which illustrates that this class of variety is concerned with the attitudes of greater or less formality. Finally, in describing *Attitudes according to interference* Quirk and his co-authors touch upon mixtures of variety (e.g. a foreign accent with Standard English, educated varieties of English in India, Pakistan and several African countries, and creoles and pidgins) as examples of interference varieties.

This framework of classes of varieties, together with a discussion of examples of different varieties within each class, provides a comprehensive means of referring to all the many variations that are to be observed in English. But its more important purpose is to enable the authors to indicate within the total range of possibilities those particular varieties of English—i.e. those which are found in *educated usage*—which form the target of their description. It is essential for them to acknowledge the existence of varieties and to categorize them, but they do so as a kind of ground-clearing operation in order to apply themselves to their principal task, and varieties thereafter have little importance in their description, wide-ranging and distinguished though this is.

So much, then, for these two approaches to the description of varieties—a sociolinguistic approach and a description of English approach—which have been developed independently of the particular interests of the ELT specialist. In the following chapter we shall look at varieties from our own professional standpoint.

11 Varieties of English: a TEFL approach

1. Why a Special Approach is Needed

1.1 Teachers of English as a foreign language have two special reasons for needing a framework within which the varieties of English can be understood and described, a framework moreover which is adapted to their own conditions. The first reason arises from the fact that the teachers of English, above any other group of people, are continually made aware of the existence of many different kinds of English. The profession includes among its members both non-native speakers of English and others for whom it is the mother tongue; it embraces a vast range of different 'interference varieties' among the learners, as well as different target levels and expected uses of English; above all, familiarity with English in all its manifestations is part of the stock-in-trade of the profession. A suitable framework of description is obviously required, as part of the English teacher's professional armoury.

1.2 The second reason is one which not only confirms the need for a descriptive framework for varieties of English but also suggests that the framework should be specially adapted to the requirements of the profession, rather than being borrowed from, and hence conceived in terms of, another discipline. This second reason is that the great majority of teachers of English as a foreign language receive an education and a professional training which contain no sociolinguistics and no deep study of the English language. Consequently they are not intellectually prepared for the kinds of reasoning employed in the two types of approach outlined in the previous chapter.

1.3 This deficiency of preparation has nothing to do with intelligence, nor is it necessarily linked with the teacher's general level of education. Teachers are, by definition, members of the better-educated segments of the community, and they are as intelligent as members of the other professions. The lack of preparation is of two particular kinds, one of which makes it difficult for the English teacher to understand the sociolinguistic approach, while the other relates to the 'description of English' approach.

1.4 In the case of sociolinguistics, the difficulty is that sociolinguistics is a *science*: in particular, one of the social sciences. That very fact means that sociolinguistics assumes on the part of those who study it certain attitudes towards data, observation, generalizations, hypotheses, experiments, the use of mathematics and statistics, the ultimate desirability of arriving at theoretical statements, as well as other features of science. But teachers of English are educated and trained in the *humanities*, above all in English literature, where their intellectual talents are directed towards ideas of beauty, to developing responses to a writer's ideas, to acquiring a subtle appreciation of nuances in a text, and so on. The Arts-trained teacher can rarely make the leap into the different intellectual game which is Science, without receiving (or obtaining by his own efforts) some special preparation for the task, and this special preparation is available only for the small minority of teachers who are able to take specialist and postgraduate courses.

1.5 In the case of the 'description of English' approach to varieties the difficulty for the average teacher of English is less severe than in the case of the sociolinguistic approach. The long tradition of studies in the English language is rooted in the humanities rather than the sciences. Nevertheless the rigour and depth of such studies as, for example, the *Grammar of Contemporary English* by Quirk and others, is greater than most teachers are exposed to during their training. To take an apparently trivial point, the use of unfamiliar terminology and the proliferation of technical terms is a characteristic of all advanced studies, simply because such studies are bound to make distinctions and to state relationships of ever-greater subtlety and generality, and in so doing they quickly go beyond the limits of everyday vocabulary. Yet many teachers of English shy away from the use in their own discipline of technical terms, are quickly put off by unfamiliar words, and believe themselves to be intellectually unready for the terminology of powerful description. This is particularly true in the area of grammar, which is often so badly taught in schools and colleges that many teachers of English are left with a strong antipathy towards its terms, its categories and even its nature. And so, even for the task of understanding a humanities-based 'description of English' approach, the preparation received by most teachers of English is insufficiently rigorous. An approach is needed which does not expect of the teacher the kind of intellectual jump which faces him in a sociolinguistic or 'description of English' approach to varieties. What follows is an outline of such a 'TEFL approach'. (The description of varieties in this chapter incorporates insights derived from the work of J. R. Firth, D. Abercrombie, J. C. Catford, A. McIntosh, M. A. K. Halliday, R. Quirk, and W. F. Mackey, to all of whom I am indebted for much of my professional understanding.)

2. Some Basic Assumptions

2.1 All languages exhibit both change and diversity. The details of change and diversity described in this chapter, although they follow generally applicable principles, are specific to English.

2.2 The diversity exhibited in all languages can be summarized, for practical purposes (e.g. those of the EFL teacher) under three headings:

(i) *Varieties relating to differences of USER* (i.e. the speaker or writer);

(ii) *Varieties relating to differences of USE* (i.e. the theme, subject, purpose, communicative intention, etc.);

(iii) *Varieties relating to differences of SOCIAL RELATIONS* (i.e. roughly, the degree of formality existing between speaker/writer and those he is addressing, or which is inherent in the situation).

3. The Analysis

1. Varieties relating to differences of USER
The kinds of information conveyed

3.1 The individual human being normally reflects his identity in his speech and writing, and in particular he provides information about (a) his *geographical origins*, and (b) his *social and educational history*. (He also normally expresses other facets of his individuality such as sex, age-range, body size, temperament, etc., but these particular personal characteristics are not relevant to a model of the varieties of English and will be ignored in this analysis.) Of course the individual can disguise his origins, although it is more difficult to do so than many people realize. But the essential fact is that whenever a person writes or speaks he provides information of some kind about these two facets of his identity; and the listener or reader responds and reacts to this information, whether he is conscious of doing so or not.

3.2 Information about geographical origins
This kind of information relates to two different distinctions: (i) the particular branch of the 'language family' of English that the speaker or writer belongs to; (ii) his use of a particular regional (or non-regional) dialect and accent. The first of these distinctions locates him broadly within the world-wide population of English-users, while the second distinction locates him more precisely within a major geographical area and also provides a link with the social and educational dimension.

3.3 The 'language family' of English
Every language acquires in the course of time evidence of the history of those who speak and use it. Migrations, contact with other societies and languages, major social and political changes within the population,

changing functions for which the language is used, sheer numbers of users, the simple passage of time—all these factors, and others, influence a language and tend to produce diversity within it. In the case of English, the history of English-speaking peoples is reflected, among other ways, in the great geographical dispersion of English over the world, and above all in the gradual growth of two principal branches of English—a 'British English' branch and an 'American English' branch —each with its own off-shoots. The family as a whole is illustrated in Diagram 6.

3.4 The intention of the diagram is to illustrate in graphic form the existence of very many different kinds of English, in the sense that the speakers of each recognize fellow-members of that community by their English, and knowingly distinguish themselves from users of other kinds of English on that basis. But the diagram is also intended to show other affinities, especially those by which users of American English and users of British English recognize and identify each other. (P. Strevens, *British and American English.* See also Chapter 12.) Canadian English is more like United States English than is, e.g., Australian English; West African English is more like British English than is, e.g., Samoan English. These affinities reflect past history and present affiliations, in varying quantity; in the case of areas where English is used but is not the native language it is quite possible that affiliations could change—as for example where American English is imported on a large scale into an educational system which has previously been oriented solely towards British English, thereby creating among the younger generation an orientation towards American English which their parents did not possess.

3.5 Past and present varieties

Languages change with time. At a given point in history, a given language will possess within itself diversity of the kinds we are discussing—in the case of English, there is a history of more than two centuries during which the branches of the family of English have been establishing themselves. And since languages change with time and since languages are the sum of their varieties, varieties also change with time. But the rules which govern language changes (whatever the rules may be, and accepting that our knowledge of them is insufficient for us to be able to predict future changes) are such that varieties themselves may change differently from each other, may merge or diverge, may change faster or more slowly. In discussing historical forms of English, the term *état de langue* is used to refer to 'the state of the language' at a particular historical period. We can know relatively little about past forms of English, and all the discussion of varieties which follows is concerned with the present-day language—with varieties of contemporary English.

DIAGRAM 6

The Language Family of English

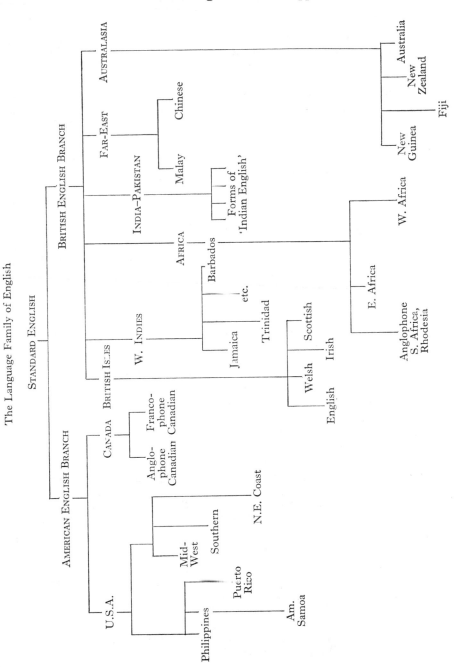

3.6 Dialects and accents

These two terms are deliberately used, in this analysis of varieties, with separate and distinct meanings. The community of people who use English make up a world-wide body of several hundreds of millions of people. Within that total body there exist smaller communities whose English possesses community characteristics of grammar, vocabulary and pronunciation, and who recognize fellow-members by their use of these characteristics—for instance, as being a New Zealander, in particular a Maori; or as being from Britain, from Scotland, with more rather than less education, and not Anglicized; and so on. Forms of English with community characteristics—which may be geographical or social, or a mixture of all three—are known as *dialects* and *accents*. Where the special identifying features are solely a matter of pronunciation, the form is an *accent*; where the identifying features are *grammatical and/or lexical*, the form is a *dialect*.

It follows from this definition that any and every form of English spoken or written by anyone anywhere in the world can be identified as being one dialect or another, and if spoken, as one accent or another. This definition rejects the popular idea of a dialect being anything that is not 'standard': on the contrary, in this view the standard form, too, is a dialect, and is spoken with some accent or another. The positive advantages of defining *dialect* and *accent* in this way will become clear shortly.

3.7 Examples of dialects and accents

3.7.1 A great many teachers and learners of English know only Standard English (see later) and a non-regional accent, so that they may find it difficult to imagine what other dialects and accents are like. Accent differences are the easiest to refer to, though not to indicate on the printed page. Standard English can be spoken with any accent, and it is commonly heard with an accent from either a British or an American branch of the English family. (See Chapter 9.)

3.7.2 Dialect differences we should recall, are lexical, or grammatical, or both. Lexical (i.e. vocabulary) differences include different names for the same object in different places (e.g. a *cow-shed, byre, cow-house,* etc.; an *earwig, golliker, forkietail,* etc.; a *lane, ginnel, snicket,* etc.;) and also different 'grammatical' words (e.g. *happen,* for *perhaps*; *thisen* for *yourself*; *aye* and *nay* for *yes* and *no*; *nowt* for *nothing*, and *owt* for *something/anything*; etc.).

3.7.3 A phrase which is in Yorkshire dialect but is nevertheless well known in Britain is the following:

> If ever tha does owt for nowt, always do it
>   for thisen.
>
> (If you ever do something for nothing, always
>   do it for yourself.)

3.7.4 There is of course far more to the description of local dialects than can be shown in this chapter. It is worth remembering that for great numbers of people the dialect of English they learn to speak and understand in childhood is a local or regional dialect and accent; and for them, that is what English *is*. It is only later, usually at school, that they are introduced to Standard English as the socially-agreed vehicle for educated use and international communication.

3.8 Geographical and social/educational dialects and accents

3.8.1 As we noticed in section 1 above, the varieties of English which identify a particular user convey information about his geographical origins and about his social and educational history. It is sometimes said that English possesses 'geographical dialects' and 'social dialects', as if one particular set of dialects (and accents) conveyed one kind of information while a different set convey the other kind. Even if that was true until, say, 1930, the reality nowadays is considerably more complex than that. It is certainly possible to make some general statements about *geographical* information, however. First, and confining ourselves to areas of the world where English is the mother tongue, every region has associated with it a particular dialect and accent. Sometimes a single city, or a town, or a small locality, also possesses its own identifiable dialect and accent. Second, these 'regional' and 'local' dialects and accents are always associated in the following way: a person who uses a particular regional dialect uses *only* the equivalent accent; but the regional accent may be used with a 'non-regional' dialect. Third, it follows that the dialect of region X and the accent of region Y are *never* associated, only dialect X and accent X, and dialect Y with accent Y. (Yorkshire dialect with a Scottish accent, for instance, does not happen.) Fourth, certain 'non-regional' dialects can be spoken with *any* regional accent. Finally, each main geographical area of the English-speaking world possesses one or more relatively 'non-regional' accent, which is used *only* when the dialect being used is also non-regional. Thus the geographical information a person supplies about himself is conveyed either (i) by regional dialect and associated accent; or (ii) by regional accent, the dialect being of a non-regional kind. Or geographical information can be absent, as when a non-regional dialect and non-regional accent are both used.

3.8.2 What of social and educational information? The first point to notice is that until half a century ago, in Britain at least, the two were largely the same, since superior education was available only to those in a higher social class: the membership of the 'superior education' group automatically presupposed membership of the 'upper-class' group—though the converse was not necessarily true. Within the past fifty years, however, education at all levels including the highest has increasingly become available to all members of the community, and so the possession of superior educational attainments is no longer associated with membership of any particular social class, and social attitudes towards dialect and accent have altered radically as a consequence.

3.8.3 How was the information 'upper class' conveyed in the earlier period when it was not differentiated from the information 'superior education'? The answer is, by the use of one particular dialect, *Standard English*, and of a socially-marked version of one of the non-regional accents: in Britain usually the accent known as *Received Pronunciation*, or *RP*. It is to these non-regional dialects and accents that we should now turn.

3.9 Standard English: the universal non-regional dialect.

3.9.1 By contrast with the regional and local dialects, which have currency only in their areas of origin and are linked in the spoken language exclusively with the appropriate regional and local accent, there exists in English one particular dialect which (to state its negative feature first) has no affinity either with a particular region or with a particular accent. But this dialect has six important positive features:

   (i) it is used by educated people who make use of English all over the world, not solely in Britain;

  (ii) wherever it is used, it displays virtually no geographical or social variation; (though see Chapter 9 for distinctive characteristics of British and American English);

 (iii) it may be spoken with an accent from *any* geographical locality, or with a non-regional accent;

 (iv) it has been universally accepted in the English-speaking world as the only appropriate model for educational use (and hence, for 'educated' use) whether we are thinking of English as the mother tongue or as a foreign or second language;

  (v) it is the variety of English which has been the most comprehensively described and studied;

 (vi) it is the dialect of literature, with exceptions only for works that deliberately introduce and emphasize local features of language. This dialect is known as *Standard English*.

3.9.2 There are three important comments to be made about Standard English. The first concerns the meaning of 'standard'. As a descriptive term, 'standard' has the meaning 'used by the majority of people designated'. The people designated in the definition are those who are concerned with education, with educated usage, with literature. It is certainly not true that the majority of all users of English, not even the majority of all native speakers of English, use Standard English dialect. But it certainly *is* true that the majority of educated usage in English— virtually one hundred per cent of it—is conducted in Standard English. (Those native speakers of English who have worked abroad as teachers or administrators or missionaries, during the past century or so have almost invariably been, by definition, educated people and hence users of Standard English dialect. Since these people have been the only native speakers of English encountered by the populations of India, Africa and Asia where they have worked, it is widely assumed by these populations that *all* native users of English employ Standard English, and they are consequently much surprised, on first visiting Britain or the United States (for example) to discover that the majority of the population does not use Standard English all the time, if at all, particularly in speech.)

3.9.3 The second observation is that Standard English is the name of a *dialect*, not an *accent*. The characteristics of Standard English are displayed when it is written down, and also in a transcript of speech; but when a person speaks English using Standard English dialect he is bound to use one accent or another, and this may be either a non-regional accent (in the same way that Standard English is a non-regional dialect) or a regional accent. As we shall see later, the fact that non-regional Standard English dialect is *often* spoken with a non-regional accent does not mean that this is *always*, or even *necessarily*, the case. Indeed, in Britain at present there is a perceptible tendency to favour the use of an accent which displays a person's regional origins. A similar tendency accounts for the emergence, in some countries where English is a second language, of a common usage among members of the educated population, consisting of Standard English with a regional or local accent.

3.9.4 The third observation is that the word *standard* as used in the term Standard English does not mean 'better'. It means simply 'most frequent' in the usage of the people referred to. A dialect that is not Standard English ought to be referred to as *non-standard*, rather than *sub-standard*. People do apply value judgments to the choice and use of one dialect rather than another, but such judgements are applied after the act of description: they are not inherent in the descriptive facts. Descriptively speaking, Standard English dialect, as a variety of English, is neither 'better' nor 'worse' than Cornish dialect, or the dialect of Indiana, or Black English, or Scots. What must be remembered is that a person's language is part of his identity and part of his culture.

3.9.5 There are a great many circumstances where argument rages over the relative merits of different approaches to language education, and over the wisdom or otherwise of expecting young people to adopt a dialect or accent which they have not grown up with. These arguments are complicated ones, often with overtones of bitterness as between one social class, or racial group, or cultural affinity, and another. The specialist in the description of English can contribute to the arguments the observation that, whatever the convenience or appropriateness or frequency of any particular dialect in a given situation, considered as varieties all are equally valuable: they are all expressions of human individuality and human society.

3.10 Non-regional accents, including RP

3.10.1 If one considers the major areas where English is spoken as the mother tongue (Britain, the United States, Canada, Australia, New Zealand, for example) a tendency can be seen for one or two accents to emerge in each area which have three properties:

(i) they are used *only* in speaking Standard English (though they are not the *only* accent used with Standard English);

(ii) they are geographically more or less neutral within that area; but

(iii) they recognizably belong to that geographical area as a whole and not to any other. The adjective 'general' is often applied to accents of this type, as in General American, or General Australian. J. Windsor-Lewis prefers the term 'General British' to 'RP', and he uses the former, with its initials GB, in his *Concise Pronouncing Dictionary of British and American English*.

3.10.2 In Britain, the non-regional accent is RP (an abbreviation from the outdated term 'Received Pronunciation', where 'received' meant 'socially acceptable'; since 'received' no longer has this sense and since the 'society' which arbitrated upon what was and was not 'received' no longer exists, the term is nowadays usually referred to only by its initials, RP). It is, by definition, an accent of Britain (and not of Australia, North America etc.) with no affinity to any particular part of Britain; and it is used only in speaking Standard English. This is the pronunciation which has been more thoroughly and comprehensively described, in the literature of phonetics, than any other, and it is the one which, in default of any more obvious choice, is usually adopted as the target for foreign and Commonwealth learners of British English.

3.10.3 RP is usually described and discussed as if it were a single, invariant accent, spoken in exactly the same way by all those who speak it at all. There is some doubt whether this has ever been strictly true, but at the present time it seems that the label RP is applied to two distinct bodies of pronunciation. One of these is the descendant of the former, socially-marked RP which still serves as a marker of social class and suggests that the speaker (if male) went to a public school, to Oxford or Cambridge, or perhaps was an officer in the Army. The other body of pronunciation to which the label RP is applied says 'I am middle class' (where the other version says 'I am upper class') and it is usually associated with a rather high level of education, beyond secondary and into university or art college or polytechnic. A further feature of this version of RP is that it often retains a small amount of information about regional origins—not a broad regional or local accent, but an identifiable trace. (Accents can be more or less strongly marked: when used with Standard English they tend to be less marked; when used with the local dialect they tend to be strongly marked.) This *RP* is thus a cluster of weakly marked accents. The reasons why this has come about are complex, but among younger people the reasons include a conscious disdain of the upper class, a growing interest in the culture and tradition of the regions of Britain, and possibly a counterbalance to the deliberate but occasional use, in songs and in colloquial conversation, of catch-phrases and song-lyrics taken from international 'pop' culture, and spoken with a more-or-less American accent.

3.11 *'BBC English', 'Oxford Accent', 'King's English', etc.*

A number of popular labels have been used to refer to the combination of Standard English dialect and RP accent. 'BBC English' reflects the strict policy which the BBC followed for fifty years in selecting and training their announcers and official speakers. Until quite recently the BBC would normally employ for speaking duties only people for whom this combination, in its socially-marked form, was the norm of their upbringing. It is interesting to observe that with the growth of local radio and television services, and with the rise of regional feeling, the BBC now very frequently employs announcers whose accent indicates roots in the area where they are working: an identifiable measure of Welsh accent for broadcasting from Cardiff or Bangor; an identifiable character of Scottishness for Glasgow or Edinburgh; and so on.

And at the same time, on its national services the BBC has begun to make use of disc jockeys who handle the music and language of pop culture in a semi-American accent—not surprisingly, since an American accent is a world-wide feature of the language of pop. (Interestingly, international pop also departs from Standard English in some features of grammar. E.g. 'I don't want no one but you.' 'Can't take my eyes off of you' etc. But that is a separate issue.)

The term 'Oxford Accent' is now rarely used, since the period in the nineteen-thirties, when many undergraduates affected a noticeably marked version of RP, is past and forgotten. The term 'King's English' (or 'Queen's English') is a non-technical term generally used for referring to some supposed 'better' form of English, during arguments about correctness of usage in grammar or pronunciation. It has no agreed meaning as a descriptive term, and is best avoided.

3.12 *Second-language varieties, creoles and pidgins*

3.12.1 In discussing those varieties of English which convey information about the individual user of the language, the speaker or writer, we have so far confined our remarks to dialects and accents of English used by native speakers of English. There exists in addition a large number of what Quirk calls 'interference varieties': those in which some kind of contact with other languages makes itself evident. They are of three main kinds: second-language varieties; pidgins; creoles.

3.12.2 Second-language varieties

There are many countries where English, though not the mother tongue of the inhabitants, is used by a great many of them for administration, business, the law, education, etc. Most of the independent countries which are still or were formerly members of the Commonwealth fall into this category. In these countries differences may be observed in accent, or dialect, or both, and the extent of the differences ranges from a slight local accent at one extreme, to total lack of mutual intelligibility with other users of English, at the opposite extreme.

3.12.3 Second-language varieties which use Standard English with a local accent are fairly common. Labels such as 'Educated West African English', or 'Educated Singapore English' refer to varieties of this kind (see R. Tongue, *The English of Singapore and Malaysia*), and it should be noticed that the varieties they refer to are generally regarded as desirable badges of identity—as shared community characteristics and as something to be proud of. For this reason they seem to be suitable for adoption as the educational norm; teachers then feel that they are teaching English for use in their own area, not as an attempt to produce imitation British or American children.

3.12.4 Where the *dialect* used in a second-language variety is not Standard English—i.e. when there are major differences in grammar and vocabulary—the situation presents more difficulty to the teacher of English. The commonest example that is quoted is 'Indian English'. However, the term is a misleading one, since it refers not to a single variety but to a set of many varieties across the whole spectrum. The Indian (or Pakistani) doctor who communicates easily in English with professional colleagues at an international medical conference is using a type of 'Indian English' similar to those mentioned above, in which Standard English dialect is spoken with a regional accent. The Indian clerk who uses English constantly in his daily life for communicating with other Indians, by correspondence or telephone, may employ an 'Indian English' in which the dialect is not Standard English and the accent is regional or local. The lorry-driver who uses English occasionally, as a lingua franca, may be using an 'Indian English' which is for all practical purposes a pidgin. It is the second of these three examples which constitutes the typical 'Indian English' and which most frequently attracts the criticism of the teaching profession. But is criticism justified? The ultimate test of effectiveness of a variety of language is whether it meets the communication needs of those who use it. Clearly, 'Indian English' of this second type would not be adequate for the professional man to communicate with an international audience, but it probably does serve local needs well enough, just as all local dialects and accents do.

3.13 Pidgins and creoles

3.13.1 These may be regarded as 'mixed' languages resulting from prolonged contact between different cultures: we are concerned with cases where one of the ingredients in the mixture is English. Pidgins are not spoken as a mother tongue by anybody, and they usually lack some of the grammatical features of English, and have a rather small vocabulary. That does not mean that pidgins cannot be used to express a great deal: on the contrary, they are flexible, adaptable and expressive. They tend to be restricted in the kinds of activity for which they are used—for trading, or domestic service, or travel, and often across a great geographical area, such as the whole of West Africa, or over much of South-East Asia and the islands of the South-West Pacific. But they are not to be underestimated, and there is no reason to despise them.

3.13.2 The usefulness of teaching pidgin English instead of Standard English has been much debated in areas (e.g. New Guinea) where pidgin is current and where facilities for education are insufficient. If pidgin really does satisfy the communication needs of the children concerned as they grow into adult citizens, this may be a defensible policy; but if it is in fact a brush-off, a cheaper alternative to learning English, or even if it is simply felt by the people concerned to be so, then the policy may turn out to be untenable.

3.13.3 Creole languages are languages with an element of English (e.g. Krio in Sierra Leone), are full languages in the sense that they are spoken as the mother tongue by a population of people, and are used for the full range of human communication within that society. There is much to be said for dropping the term 'creole', since all it really means is 'mixed', and it is used here only in order to make this point. By that criterion English is also a creole, containing elements of German, French and Latin. The only important feature of such languages, within the perspective of a chapter on varieties of English, is that they possess already a number of features of English, and to that extent the learning of English by speakers of a creole may be somewhat easier than for a speaker of another language.

3.14 Judgments of geographical and socio-educational characteristics

Summarizing the dimensions which are used in English for the purpose of making judgments about a user of English—a person speaking or writing it—we can see that they are surprisingly few in number. They are, in fact: 'language family' identity (British, American, etc.); dialect, especially whether Standard English or not; and accent, especially whether non-regional or not. These dimensions form the basis of judgments in the following way: (a) judgments about where a person comes from are made principally on 'language family' information, dialect if not Standard English, and accent; (b) judgments on social and educational characteristics are made principally on whether Standard English is used or not, and the degree of non-regional character to the accent used.

3.15 The foregoing will serve as a summary of varieties of English which reflect differences of the individual writer or speaker: varieties of USER. We turn now to varieties relating to subject-matter, occupation, communicative role, etc.: to varieties of USE.

II *Varieties relating to differences of USE*

4.1 The kinds of variety which we are now considering are, e.g., the English of a legal document, of disc jockeys, of deep-sea fishing, of 'serious' journalism, of television horse racing commentaries, of cookery books, of chemical engineering, of literary criticism, of knitting patterns, of weather forecasts, of political oratory, of mathematics, of nineteenth century lyric poetry, etc.

4.2 One might jump to the conclusion that these varieties of use (for which the term *registers* is commonly employed) are differentiated solely by different technical vocabulary, since words or expressions like *hereinafter referred* or *freehold* or *barratry* belong chiefly in legal registers, while *golden oldie, jingle, top twenty* or *swinging sound* tend to identify the speech of the disc jockey, and *otterboard, cod end, fishing ground, icing conditions* or *shoot the trawl* are characteristics of the register of deep-sea fishing, to take only three illustrations. But register differences cannot be ascribed solely to vocabulary. The differences are almost always carried by a mixture of features of *grammar* and *pronunciation*, as well as of *vocabulary*, the mix being different in each case. The point can be illustrated by choosing in turn registers where the principal identifying features belong to one or other of these types.

4.3 Registers identified chiefly by features of grammar

4.3.1 The register of *newspaper headlines* is an example of a variety of English so familiar that its grammatical implications are usually overlooked. But (i) BRITONS BATTLE CRAZY ANT PERIL, (ii) CITY FIRE DEATH PROBE SHOCK, and (iii) ARCHBISHOP ILL: MISSES FUNERAL are all authentic pieces of English having grammatical rules that are far from universal within English. To take only some of the most obvious features, in (i) the sentence contains a subject, a verb agreeing in number (in the normal way) with the verb, and an object, but the simple present tense (BRITONS) BATTLE has a special meaning here, different from its customary 'habitual' meaning as in *dogs chase rabbits*, or *fishermen wear seaboots*. The register carries the convention that BATTLE here means 'on a particular occasion', 'in the story which you may read below this headline'. A further grammatical feature is that the articles (*a, the*) are rarely used in headlines, while long nominal groups without a main verb, as in CITY FIRE DEATH PROBE SHOCK, also display a convention which is grammatical in nature. There is much more that could be said in a detailed study of the register of newspaper headlines: the point being made is simply that grammatical features are prominent among its characteristics.

4.3.2 Legal registers (there are probably more than one, given the great range of the study and application of law) also contain grammatical features. A bill of sale for a ship reads as follows:

'I the undersigned (hereinafter called "the Transferor") in consideration of the sum of seven thousand five hundred pounds paid to me by the Joint Owners (hereinafter called "the Transferees") the Receipt of which is hereby acknowledged, transfer sixty-four shares in the Ship above particularly described, and in her boats and appurtenances, to the said Transferees.

Further I the said Transferor for myself and my heirs covenant with the said Transferees and their assigns, that I have power to transfer in manner aforesaid the premises hereinbefore expressed to be transferred, and that the same are free from encumbrances.

In witness whereof I have hereunto subscribed my name and affixed my seal on November 15. 1974.'

This text contains, obviously, several legal terms, like *appurtenances, encumbrances, assigns,* etc. But items like *whereof* and *hereunto* and *hereinafter* have a grammatical function, while expressions such as *above particularly described, in manner aforesaid, the same are,* and others require special grammatical rules: they are not produced by the grammar of Standard English outside the legal register.

4.4 *Registers identified chiefly by features of pronunciation*
The fact that some registers require special pronunciations is recognized by comedians, who can produce laughable results by either using the special pronunciation of a given register outside its normal context (for example, by imitating a clergyman's 'liturgical' pronunciation—sometimes called 'Parsonical voice'—when speaking to his housekeeper about his laundry) or *not* using the special pronunciation of a register when it is normally expected (for example, by commentating on a horse-race in the tones of everyday conversation). Among the registers where special pronunciation features are used are: sports commentaries on radio and television; oratory and public speaking; many kinds of television advertisements; poetry speaking; flight announcements at airports; tobacco auctioneering;—and one must not forget lovemaking, which can be disastrous if the tempo, voice, quality intonation and other features appropriate to the register are not adequately performed.

4.5 *Registers identified chiefly by features of vocabulary*
This is the most obvious characteristic of registers, as for example across the whole range of science and technology. The register of a

particular subject or occupation embraces its technical terms, and can be identified by them. Thus if we see a text containing terms like *DNA* or *gene* or *chromosome* we may recognize a field within biology; from *occlusion, jet-stream, front, inversion, strato-cumulus* we may recognize the register of meteorology; from *cylinder, piston, ignition, carburettor, valve, crankshaft,* etc. we may recognize a branch of automobile engineering. At the same time we should remember that vocabulary is hardly ever the sole indicator of a register: there is almost always a mixture of features in vocabulary, grammar and pronunciation.

4.6 Registers, then, are varieties which reflect different uses of the language, and they are recognized or employed in the ways we have outlined.

III *Varieties relating to different SOCIAL RELATIONS*

5.1 We select the precise formulation of what we are saying or writing according to a number of factors, and one of these is the relationship between ourselves and those we are addressing. Sometimes we are not addressing ourselves to an individual, and then it may be a degree of formality or informality vested in the situation which helps us to select our 'wording'. To take a trivial example, when I offer a cup of tea to my family in bed in the morning what I say is necessarily different from what I say if I offer a cup of tea at mid-morning to a postgraduate student, and it is different again from what I say if the Vice-Chancellor passes by in the afternoon and I offer a cup of tea to him.

5.2 These different choices are not forced upon us: they are not *determined* by the situation, only *influenced* by it. And even the degree of influence is variable. I can be coldly formal with my secretary and jovially pally with my Vice-Chancellor, if I wish. But the point is that alternatives do exist and that in choosing one rather than another we are likely to take into account the relations between ourselves and those we are addressing, as well as the nature of the situation. In so doing we are simply operating in the domain of language a range of possible patterns of social behaviour that are open to us in our life from moment to moment.

5.3 In selecting the particular kind of language, written or spoken, that the individual regards as best suited to his purpose (from this point of view) he operates a wide range of choices in vocabulary, grammar, pronunciation, tempo, range of voice pitch, voice quality, and several more dimensions. To take an example, consider the style in which this chapter—indeed, this book—is written. The style has been selected quite deliberately because the author is writing for fellow-professionals, mostly unknown to him personally, with probable expectations on their part of a fairly formal kind of language. In the next paragraph, the style will be different.

5.4 Well, now, I don't know what *you* think about it, but *I* think it's time we had some examples. It's pages and pages—or at least, that's what it feels like to me—since we last had any concrete examples in front of us. So let's do that. OK. But the trouble is, I've got to *invent* my own examples, because there really aren't any of anybody else's that I can refer you to. Still there's one set of examples that I've used with my students over the years. It seems to work fairly well: at least, chaps always reckoned they found them helpful, so let's have a go.

5.5 In the preceding paragraph the language used was deliberately chosen from an informal, colloquial, spoken style, such as the author would use when talking to a close friend or member of the family. It does not represent the extremes of familiarity, any more than *this* paragraph represents the opposite extreme of formality. But the contrast will serve as an introduction to a set of examples loosely based on the categories put forward by M. Joos, (*The Five Clocks*). He suggested that English makes use of five 'styles', which he labelled FROZEN–FORMAL–CONSULTATIVE–CASUAL–INTIMATE.

5.6 In order to provide a single situation and a single message, and to vary only the social relations and degree of formality bearing on the spcaker, imagine a large meeting that is about to start. The hall quietens down ready for proccedings to begin, all except one young lady at the back of the hall who is quite oblivious of the fact that her loud chatter is holding up the start of the meeting. What would be said to her? Using Joos's suggested labels, the following alternatives are suggested:

FROZEN style: (Anonymously, over the public address loudspeaker)
'Miss Smith must keep silent!'

FORMAL style: (Addressed by a person in authority)
'Kindly stop talking now, Miss Smith.'

CONSULTATIVE style:
'Do you mind not talking now, Miss Smith?'

CASUAL style:
'Better not talk now, Mary.'

INTIMATE style:
'Darling—shhh!'

5.7 We have now nearly reached the limits of what can be offered to the EFL teacher by way of guidance in the choice of varieties, because the profession still lacks a comprehensive study of the different kinds of alternative, displaying different degrees of formality, that are open to the user of English. Even the above five-level description does not tell the whole story: it is both too detailed for some circumstances and not detailed enough for others. It is too detailed in the sense that some kinds of discourse—legal register, for example—may not lend themselves to so many sub-divisions. It is not detailed enough in the sense that some other kinds of discourse may be yet more subtly sub-divided. And what of invective, insult, swearing, bad language? For the moment the most important task of the teacher is to be aware of the dimension, to observe the kinds of language-choice that relate to it, and to build his observations into his teaching. As more and more teaching materials are published which incorporate insights of this kind, the task will become easier.

6 *Conclusion.* In this chapter we have summarized the description of varieties of English in a way that brings in most of the phenomena (such as Standard English, dialects and accents, regional and non-regional varieties, geographical and social information, registers, degrees of formality) which are relevant to the teacher of English as a foreign language and are frequently encountered in his professional work. And the description has been deliberately expressed in terms that are accessible to the Arts-trained teacher.

Two final comments are necessary. First, this has been only an outline. The full story of varieties of English is a good deal more complex than this. And secondly, I would encourage the teacher who has followed the preceding outline to read further in the subject. Let him (or her) make a serious effort to follow the appropriate section of Quirk and others' *Grammar of Contemporary English*, and then to read some of the sociolinguistics literature on varieties. Because the 'intellectual gap' referred to at the beginning of this chapter is largely a chimera, which will vanish—or at least be seen as something capable of being leapt across—if the teacher makes a determined and serious effort to read what specialists in other disciplines have to say about diversity and variety in English.

12 British and American English

Of all the many kinds of difference that exist among the myriad varieties of English, few give rise to fiercer discussion and greater speculation than those which differentiate British and American English. Both form part of the 'family' of English summarized in Diagram 6 in Chapter 11, p. 133. Speakers of the one immediately recognize speakers of the other as being fellow English-speakers, and yet also as members of a distinct culture. In this chapter we shall contrast the two forms of the language.

Native speakers of English learn early in life that their mother tongue is written and spoken in very different ways on opposite sides of the Atlantic. It is natural that they should seek to explain, describe, and understand the origin and nature of this phenomenon. But since language is highly complex, and since the information on which to form an opinion presents itself only piecemeal, they rarely reach a satisfactory understanding. The similarities and differences between British and American English can be seen in perspective if one notices, first, that both have a common origin in English of the Elizabethan period, although their subsequent history and development have been separate and they now express and embody two cognate but distinct cultures; second, that both 'British English' and 'American English' are labels attached to a great many different varieties of English rather than to single, homogeneous entities, and that some of these varieties exhibit greater similarity than others; and third, that for purposes of education, whether English is the mother tongue or a foreign language, equivalent varieties of American or British English are used in which the similarities are maximal whereas the differences are minimal and largely confined to pronunciation.

It is customary to think of English before about 1700 as being one language ,with no specifically American characteristics yet visible, since the British settlements were so young and so small. It is after this date that the history and development of English in America began to diverge from that of English in Great Britain, because of the geographical isolation of the settlers, their growing feelings of social and political independence, their intimate contact with American Indian, Spanish, and French cultures, and their assimilation of a large population of former slaves and of great numbers of immigrants of diverse linguistic and cultural origins. Undoubtedly this separate development and the distinctive American culture which it produced were sufficient to ensure separate modes of speech and writing. But the rate of change of the language was greater than one would expect on the basis of contemporary experience, for two reasons: (1) there was no such thing as a single Elizabethan English, so that among the early settlers there existed a wide range of dialects and accents, reflecting the diversity of forms of Elizabethan English but offering no single form from which deviations could be charted; and (2) in the early eighteenth century there existed few of the pressures for standardization and conformity in speech and writing—such as universal literacy, a large literature, the media of press, radio, and television—which in Britain and North America today slow down the innate tendency for English, like all languages, to change. (Differences between English in the United States and in Canada are such as to be indistinguishable to most speakers of English from other parts of the world. In this article 'American English' embraces both the U.S. and Canadian varieties.)

During the first 200 years of separate development, one of the most striking features specific to English in America was the large number of borrowings from other cultures. For example: from the American Indian came *hickory, hooch, totem,* and *squaw;* from French came *prairie, depot, cache,* and *rotisserie;* from Spanish came *bronco, rodeo, patio,* and *vigilante;* from Dutch and German came *boss, dumb* (meaning stupid), and *Santa Claus;* and from African came *gumbo, voodoo,* and *okra* (see Marckwardt 1958; Mencken 1963).

The contemporary situation, then, is one of two distinct yet cognate cultures in Britain and America, each possessing a form of English as the mother tongue. The differences of vocabulary, grammar, pronunciation, orthography, semantics, and usage between the two reflect both the similarities and the differences between the cultures.

Differences. There are three main methods of describing the nature of the differences between American and British English. In the past it was customary to concentrate on words, using them to illustrate differences of borrowings, of historical change, and of distinctions in meaning. In descriptions of word differences, the treatment of grammar and pronunciation is fairly superficial (Mencken 1963). The examples given above illustrate the first method of description. More recently there have been written descriptions of each kind of English in terms of grammar, vocabulary, pronunciation, and sometimes orthography which treat the language more systematically than do word-based descriptions. A third method of description is to see each form of English as comprising a constellation of varieties, which differ in particular ways according to the speaker or writer, his purpose, and his immediate situation.

Vocabulary. The examples which follow are but a small selection of the total number of contrasting vocabulary items. It is assumed in each case that the English being described, unless otherwise stated, is that of an educated man dealing in everyday discourse. The items illustrate the case where there are different British and American words for the same idea and also the case where one form of English has only one word but the other form has two or more words. The length of the list of different words does not indicate a degree of nonunderstanding between British and American English. Few of these items cause anything but the most ephemeral pause in comprehension; neither do they constitute a major learning task.

The following words are a part of the educated speaker's general vocabulary (American words are given first): *closet–cupboard; cookie–biscuit; elevator–lift; janitor–caretaker; mailman–postman; patrolman–constable; phonograph–gramophone; railroad–railway; sidewalk–pavement; vacation–holiday* (and others); *shorts* (men's)–*underpants; undershirt–vest; vest–waistcoat; sneakers–pumps, canvas shoes; someplace–somewhere.* The next examples are a part of the educated speaker's vocabulary of the automobile (American words are again given first): *automobile–motor-car; gas, gasoline–petrol; fender–wing, mudguard; hood–bonnet; trunk–boot; windshield–windscreen; sedan–saloon; trailer–caravan.* The following examples illustrate the case where one form of English has more than one word and the other has only one to express an idea (American words first): *baggage–luggage* (personal to the traveller), *baggage* (of travellers in general); *a movie–a film; the movies–the pictures; expressway, freeway, parkway, thruway, turnpike, superhighway–motorway.* (These last American terms are used in different parts of the United States to refer to limited-access trunk roads.)

Grammar. The underlying grammatical rules of any language (not the grammarian's formulation of how one should use it, but the internalized, unverbalized rules according to which sentences are created) are more crucial yet fewer in number than its vocabulary items. Consequently, there are a smaller number of grammatical differences between American English (AE) and British English (BE) than vocabulary differences. Indeed, it may be only the combination of an unfamiliar word with an unfamiliar pattern of grammar that causes a hesitation in comprehension, rather than the isolated occurrence of either. For example, an Englishman understands an American talking about his *vacation* (BE, *holiday*); but in a sentence like the AE, *Did you have your vacation yet?* (BE, *Have you had your holiday yet?*) the unfamiliar item, *vacation*, in the unfamiliar pattern of grammar may require a longer semantic decoding time.

N.O.—11a

The following examples are intended to suggest that most grammatical differences between AE and BE are relatively trivial, in addition to being few in number. American English sometimes employs one more word than does British English in a particular syntactic item (American items are given first): he's in *the* hospital–he's in hospital; all *of* those solutions—all those solutions; to visit *with* someone—to visit someone. Less frequently, British English employs one more word than does American English (American item first): to stay home—to stay *at* home; what day is today?—what day is *it* today?

The verbs *to get* and *to have* display differences, some of which can be easily stated. But usage is changing; with the exception of *gotten*, which occurs in American but never in British English, the other examples are only statistically more likely, not absolute features of the one or the other.

When *to get* means to acquire or to obtain, American English has the past participle *gotten* and British English has *got*. For example, American English has: I wish we had *gotten* a new car; and British English has: I wish we had *got* a new car.

The major difference occurs where there is a clear distinction of meaning between 'habitually' and 'in the present state' or 'at the present moment'. When habitually is meant, both American and British English use *have* alone. When the present state is meant there is a difference: American English uses *have* and British English uses *have got*. Where no such choice is implied, *have* is used in both forms of English. The question form *Do you have* is usual in American English, as against *Have you got* in British English. Where there is no clear choice between habitually and in the present state, the usage is the same. Mr Curtis *has* a meeting on Friday morning (AE and BE). In the question form, the American usage is: *Do you have* a light?; and the British usage is: *Have you* a light? or *Have you got* a light? (It must be stated, however, that the American question form *Do you have* is becoming common among the younger generation in Britain.)

The following apocryphal conversation pinpoints the chief contrast in the have–have got–get–gotten complex:

American: 'Do you have many children?'
Englishwoman: 'No, only one a year.'

Other differences appear in the use of prepositions: for example, an American would say *different than*, but an Englishman would say *different from* or (occasionally) *different to*. Also, an American would say *to check something out*, but an Englishman would say *to check something*, *to check up*, or *to check up on something*. Differences also appear in the use of the pronoun with *one*. An American would say *when one has seen it, he understands*, but an Englishman would say *when one has seen it, one understands*.

Pronunciation. The pronunciations of American and British English are basically similar; the fundamental sound patterns of BE and AE are far more like each other than they are like the sound patterns of any other language. The number of consonants is the same, permissible consonant-clusters and vowel-consonant sequences are similar, the stress and rhythm patterns are based on similar prosodic combinations of weak and strong stresses, the relation between stress and vowel-length is of the same general type, and so is the basic set of contrasting intonation 'tones'. But to list the technical similarities does not obliterate the undoubted fact that the pronunciation of English is very different on the two sides of the Atlantic.

One noticeable feature is the different treatment of the *r* sound. Thus, in the dominant educated accent of Britain the following pairs or triplets of words, and others like them, are pronounced exactly alike and with no trace of an *r* sound: *law, lore; paw, pore, pour; saw, sore, soar; maw, more; bawd, bored, board*, and so forth.

It is necessary to point out this feature, since native speakers with one accent have difficulty in grasping what actually happens in the other. British readers must realize that for American speakers of English the above list contains words with two different pronunciations: the first word in each example being without an *r* sound, the others being with an *r* sound. American readers must realize that in all the pairs of words in the above list the first and second are pronounced alike by speakers of British English, and that none of them is spoken with an *r* sound. (In Scottish and Irish accents and in some regional accents of England, however, an *r* sound is heard in these words following the vowel but not affecting its quality.)

In many other types of words, the difference is of another kind. In the examples which follow, American pronunciations invariably include an *r* sound, whereas the dominant educated accent of Britain has no *r* sound in any of them: *hurt, earth, ear, bird, worthy, beer, work, worse, pair, gurgle, furs, tear, urban, search, turf, verge, curve*, and so forth.

If the occurrence of an *r* sound differs in the two forms of English, so also does its formation and therefore its quality. In all the words listed above, no *r* sound occurs in British English. But in American English, in all words spelled with *r* there is an *r* sound which occurs simultaneously with the vowel before it. (The technical label is illuminating: the vowels in such cases are said to be *r*-coloured.) No similar sound occurs in British English, but all American speakers use it; consequently it is a diagnostic feature for identifying speakers of one form or the other. All other occurrences of *r* sounds are virtually identical in both kinds of English.

The treatment of the *t* sound also differs in American and British English. The British speaker cannot hear any difference in the following pairs of words and others like them as spoken in American English: *writer–rider*, *written–ridden*, *petal–pedal*, *catty–caddy*, *latter–ladder*, *utter–udder*, and so forth. In British English, these words would invariably be pronounced with the *t* sound in the first instance and the *d* sound in the second. Experimental evidence suggests that when these words are spoken in American English as isolated pairs of words, slight differences of vowel-length enable American speakers to recognize which word of each pair is being spoken. In connected speech, however, and to British ears, they are identical.

The vowel-systems of the two forms of English do not entirely overlap either in the quality of sound heard or in the contrasts each vowel enters into. The vowels in words like *tee*, *fall*, and *cool* are not exactly the same in AE and BE; to be more explicit one needs to invoke the descriptive categories of phonetics, since otherwise one is limited to saying that the difference between AE and BE vowels is one of sound-quality, of length, and of whether the sound-quality changes in the course of pronouncing the vowel.

However, in the perception of vowels and diphthongs lies the focus of important generalizations which the Americans and the British make about each other's speech. To English ears, American speech sounds nasal and is often pejoratively referred to as having a nasal twang. It is possible to show that a degree of nasality occurs at certain points in British English too, notably in vowels which are immediately followed by a nasal consonant (for example, in *arm*, *man*, *sing*, *bring*, and so on). But in American English nasalization occurs in much longer stretches of speech. This nasality is unremarked in America, but it is socially unacceptable to many speakers of British English. Such judgments are a matter of prejudice and have no bearing on the absolute merits of either form of English.

Americans often refer pejoratively to the clipped speech of the British, who in turn disparage the drawl of Americans. These judgments probably refer to a difference in the extent to which vowels are lengthened in strongly stressed syllables—for example, in the first syllable of *after*, *daughter*, *terrible*, and *constantly* or in the second syllable of *before*, *improve*, *control*, and so forth. The vowel of a stressed syllable is only very slightly lengthened in British pronunciation but is considerably lengthened in American pronunciation. The American, hearing less lengthening, describes British speech as clipped; the British listener, hearing more lengthening, refers to it as a drawl.

The differences that exist in the vowel and consonant systems of BE and AE account for a large proportion of the differences consciously observed or merely felt by the speakers of one form upon hearing the other. Fortunately it is an easy task to learn to make the mental compensations and readjustments that make it possible to understand the other form of English. Although it is a slow and difficult business to adjust one's output (that is, to speak with a different accent), it is easy and quick to accept an alternative input (that is, to comprehend another accent).

One further characteristic of American pronunciation that contrasts with British speech is the frequency of 'spelling pronunciations' in both place-names and proper names and the lack of stress-reductions in such words. The British speaker hears the American say *Edinburgh* with four syllables ('ed-in-bʌ-row) where he uses three ('ed-n-brə); he hears words ending in -*ham* (for example, *Buckingham*) pronounced in American English with a final syllable like the meat (-ham) when he expects a weak final syllable (-əm). It is not true, however, as many believe, that the shortening of place-names is the prerogative of the British speaker. An American does the same when he pronounces *Connecticut* or *Arkansas*. Proper names of foreign origin are usually anglicized in America but not in Britain. Thus the eminent American linguist Bernard Bloch was surprised to be addressed with a German pronunciation of his last name when visiting Britain; he was accustomed in America to its being pronounced identically with *block*.

Differences of pronunciation have been described in some detail, not only because they have often been inadequately treated in the past, but also because they carry some of the major distinctions between the two forms of English. It would be possible to add a catalogue of differences in intonation, rhythm, stress, and other features of pronunciation. But these seem to be relatively unimportant differences of detail rather than crucial systematic contrasts.

To the average person, the obvious defining characteristics of American and British English reside in the treatment of the *r* sound, the reduction (or lack of it) of *t* to *d* between voiced sounds, differences of voice-quality in an otherwise similar set of vowels, the acceptance or rejection of nasality, and a difference in the lengthening of stressed vowels. None of these constitutes a serious barrier to comprehension, but all quickly identify the speaker as being American or British.

Orthography. The list which follows includes examples of most of the types of spelling differences that distinguish the two forms of English (American spelling is given first): *aluminum–aluminium; carburetor–carburettor; catalog–catalogue; check* (money)*–cheque; color–colour; jewelry–jewellery; molded–moulded; pajamas–pyjamas; plow–plough; practice* (verb, noun)*–practise* (verb), *practice* (noun)*; pretense–pretence; theater–theatre; traveler–traveller; tire* (on wheel)*–tyre; whiskey–whisky; program–programme;* and so forth. (The spelling *program* has recently been adopted in Britain to refer to computer instructions. This gives in British English a visual differentiation between *programme* (of events) and *program* (for a computer) that is absent in American

English.) The differences of spelling are rather systematic: *pretense* (AE) but *pretence* (BE) has a parallel in *defense* (AE) but *defence* (BE); *honor* (AE) but *honour* (BE) has a parallel in *color* (AE) but *colour* (BE); *catalog* (AE) but *catalogue* (BE) has a parallel in *analog* (AE) but *analogue* (BE).

In journalism, advertising, and some other fields, a number of spelling differences occur in American as compared with British English in addition to the general types of differences illustrated above. One common case is the change of *-ight* to *-ite*: *DANCING TONITE* is common in America but rare in Britain. Also, the Chicago *Tribune* introduced a set of reformed spellings in 1935 which includes such spellings as *thru* for *through*; such spellings have come into widespread use in America. In general, British English takes a more authoritarian and conservative view of spelling, whereas American English is more willing to be adventurous and to create an effect at the expense of spelling conventions.

Varieties. In Britain and America the selection of one variety rather than another reflects, as we have seen, three dimensions: the geographical origins and the social status of the individual speaker or writer; the particular purpose for which he is speaking or writing; and the social relations between the speaker or writer and those he is addressing, especially as such relations determine the degree of formality that constrains his choice of language. (See Chapters 10 and 11.)

The individual is identified, then, by his use of particular geographical and social varieties of English. The varieties themselves are not identical in America and Britain, but exactly the same kind of distinctions are made and similar judgments are aroused in the listener or reader in both places. When one speaks or writes, one does so in one dialect or another; when one speaks, one necessarily speaks with one accent or another. Accent features are manifested in sound-patterns of various kinds; dialect differences are manifested in grammatical features and local vocabulary. 'I knowed you wasn't Oklahomy folks,' says one of John Steinbeck's characters in *The Grapes of Wrath*, thereby giving some indications of an Oklahoma accent and illustrating some grammatical and vocabulary features of an Oklahoma dialect (grammar: *I knowed* for *I knew*, *you wasn't* for *you weren't*; vocabulary: *Oklahomy* and possibly the use of *folks*).

The system of varieties outlined in Chapter 11 exists in both BE and AE, with differences only of detail.

Innovations and neologisms. Any language at any moment bears within it evidence of innovations and of archaisms as well as the great mass of what is current. In British English as in American, new words and technical terms are continually being invented and accepted. Most of these become common to both sides of the Atlantic, and the traffic is by no means as one-way as many British purists believe. If it is true that Americans are more ready than the British to invent new words and expressions, it is also true that a great many neologisms are ephemeral. In particular, some varieties of the language specialize in rapid change: only a portion of the new words and expressions of the world of teen-age pop music remain current, since it is a condition of their invention that they should identify the users as being of a given age and era. In general, languages retain those neologisms which are of lasting usefulness. This is true of both British and American English.

A consideration of the varieties of English is important for two reasons. First, the description of the differences between American and British English in terms of grammar, vocabulary, pronunciation, and orthography ignores the patterning of similarities between them in their varieties. Unlike the other descriptions, that of varieties is dynamic or operational. The study of varieties reveals that the static differences do not prevent a high degree of dynamic similarity. The second reason is that the affinities and distinctions of the British and American cultures are most clearly displayed in the varieties of the English language.

Education. Where English is the mother tongue—as in America, Britain, Australia, and the West Indies—the maximum ability to understand and to produce it is sought by teachers, using Standard English as the target dialect with some locally suitable accent. In earlier days, the procedures for inducing this command of English concentrated on stamping out all traces of local dialect and accent, learning by rote a number of grammatical prescriptions and proscriptions, cultivating an artificial sub-literary style for the writing of conventional essays, and studying a small selection of accredited works of literature. The details of these processes varied on the two sides of the Atlantic, but the general pattern was the same. It is now widely accepted that the child should not be required to give up the linguistic behaviour of his home culture but that instead he should be taught an additional dialect and accent (that is, Standard English and the educationally acceptable accent). This process of extending from the child's present base is increasingly followed elsewhere in the English syllabus. With the emergence of the concept of varieties of language, the educational aim can now be expressed as enabling the individual, by the time he finishes his education, to operate in as many different relevant varieties as possible, with the choice of varieties dictated by a general consideration of his future social, cultural, and educational needs. In all these matters, American and British practice is in broad agreement.

English as a foreign language. It is not solely in the teaching of English as the mother tongue that educational considerations arise. For millions of children and adults, the learning of English as a foreign language is a task that occupies an important part of their lives. Teaching English to speakers of other languages requires an effort on a major scale which takes three forms: a British-dependent form, an American-dependent form, and an autonomous form, locally directed, but still entailing a choice between American and British English as the model to be followed.

One major policy difference distinguishes the American-dependent from the British-dependent effort in teaching English overseas. For the American teacher, American English as written and spoken by the educated American is the obvious and only model to be followed by the learner. For the British teacher, local variation is acknowledged and in some circumstances accepted. The British flexibility is probably the result of the wide range of cultures in which BE has been taught; until recently AE has been taught in much more restricted areas, where a single speak-as-I-do policy has been workable. It has been the British experience over many decades that when an overseas territory in which English has a substantial role achieves social and political independence, changes take place in the form of English, particularly in the accent, current in that country. These variations are felt by the British to be psychologically and socially inevitable and to be analogous to those which occurred in America after the Revolution. Consequently, the British English-teaching profession is inclined (many American specialists say *too* inclined) to accept deviations in performance and the existence of (e.g.) an educated West African English, as a permissible model for educational purposes.

Evolution. The two forms of English are clearly different in describable ways. There is no way of deciding which is better in any meaningful sense: all one can say is that for an American the English of America is more appropriate and for an Englishman the English of Great Britain is more appropriate. American English innovates more readily and more markedly than does British English, but the effects of this innovation are trivial. The bulk of the differences lies in pronunciation, since the written varieties of the two are very similar. Differences of vocabulary occur, are easily learned, and reflect differences in the two cultures. Differences of grammar are very few indeed. The most important single characteristic of BE and AE is probably that of intercomprehensibility: for all their differences, Americans and British speak and write the same language. It is not necessary to translate into the other form in order to be understood.

British and American English can thus be seen as different developments from a common origin, displaying enough differences between them to permit a sense of independence in each, yet containing great overall similarities not only with each other but also with all the many other forms of English which coexist in the modern world.

Part Five

Some Technical Questions

13 Advantages and limitations of the language laboratory

The first language laboratories came into use in Britain early in the 1960's. From about 1965 they became a normal part of the teaching equipment of schools and colleges in most countries, for teaching foreign languages, including English as a foreign language.

From the earliest times of their use, language labs have aroused almost passionate feelings for or against them. Extravagant claims on their behalf, amounting to a belief that they provide an infallible and indispensable method of teaching, have been matched by extravagant criticisms of them, amounting to a denial that they can be of any help whatever to the learner or teacher. Between these extremes the average teacher has tried to find out for himself how best to make use of the lab in his own particular circumstances. After some fifteen years of experience of language labs there seems to have emerged a polarization of views which is widespread in Europe, but beyond which there can be discerned a more dispassionate opinion about the advantages and limitations of the language lab.

The polarization of views referred to in the previous paragraph is not simply a consequence of the extreme positions taken up by some teachers in advance of actual experience. It is based, rather, upon two conflicting kinds of reaction which teachers report after a period of weeks or months spent using a language lab. On the one hand there are those teachers whose enthusiasm for the language lab is grounded in success, who feel that they as teachers and their pupils as language learners have gained in their mutual activity, and that the lab provides possibilities which they are confident in using and to which they ascribe at least part of their improved success. On the other hand there are those teachers who regard their experience with the language lab as being disastrous, as contributing little or nothing to the pupils' learning, and as constituting a pernicious waste of money, time and effort. (See Chapter 14.)

How is it possible for such conflicting views of the same piece of teaching equipment to be honestly held, on the basis of experience, by members of the teaching profession? The answer to this question is doubtless a complex one, in which one must take account of teachers' prior expectations, of their attitudes towards the balance in teaching between language and literature, of personal antipathies towards machinery or pleasure in operating it, and many other factors. Nevertheless, the principal reason for the polarity of experience probably lies in one single fact: that language labs are heavily dependent, for their successful use, upon the presence of certain fundamental pre-requisites.

When all the requirements for successful use of a language lab are present, teachers tend to find the lab helpful and they become enthusiastic about its continued use. When all or most of these requirements are absent, success in teaching with the lab becomes difficult or impossible to achieve, teachers become disillusioned about labs in general, and they are unwilling to continue their efforts to gain success with the lab. After discussing with a great many teachers, in several countries, their experience and the reasons behind the views they now hold, I am convinced that when success with the lab was a practical possibility the teachers did in fact achieve it and became supporters of the lab, whereas when teachers have had to struggle with a language lab in conditions where success was unlikely or impossible (because of the absence of one of the fundamental requirements) they soon gave up the battle, became disillusioned and acquired attitudes hostile to language labs in general.

What are the fundamental pre-requisites for successful teaching with a language lab? Each is fairly obvious in itself: what is not self-evident is the mutual dependence of the three basic requirements.

Essential pre-requisites for language lab operation

1. Adequate maintenance and servicing arrangements.
2. Teachers aware not only of the mechanical operation of the equipment but also of its inherent methodological advantages and limitations.
3. Suitable recorded materials already in hand, or staff with the time, facilities and ability to produce them.

Maintenance and servicing

Language labs need to be reliable. Frequent breakdowns damage the confidence of teachers and students alike and they create frustration and annoyance. Even a tiny fault—a fuse blown, dirt on a relay switch, a plug accidentally pulled half-way out—can close down one booth or an entire lab installation until it is put right. Faults of this kind cannot be avoided: they are as inevitable in language labs as are electrical and mechanical faults in motor cars or television sets. But if help has to be summoned from outside whenever a fault occurs, then the teachers must resign themselves to the lab being out of use from time to time. There is no adequate substitute for technical help close at hand in the school, college or department.

But 'technical help' does not necessarily mean a fully-qualified electronics engineer, desirable though such a person is. The most economical acceptable solution is to employ a lab steward, on the analogy of a category of staff long employed by our colleagues in physics, chemistry and zoology. A language lab in use creates a great deal of work in clearing up after classes, preparing for the next class, checking tapes, recording, copying, editing, etc. and above all carrying out the simple routine servicing that prevents most trivial faults from occurring and cures most of the remainder. The high-powered engineer is needed only for major faults, which are fairly rare. But a lab steward (who is often a young enthusiast working up to further training) can contribute to organization, tidiness, routine 'prophylactic' servicing, and a great many essential tasks for which an electronics engineer may be almost too well-qualified.

Teachers' awareness of the advantages and limitations of the language lab
Being competent in the mechanical operation of a language lab console and booths is one thing; being aware of the lab in the wider perspective of the profession of language teaching is another. The former ability is simple to acquire, and indeed a language lab 'monitor' does not have to be a trained teacher—but in that case the monitor can contribute little or nothing to the teaching and learning except to keep the learners' attention on the job. The wider understanding is necessary if the teacher is to make full use of the potential advantages of the language lab and at the same time to avoid the pitfalls and limitations of language lab methods.

Ideally, the teacher using such methods needs to be aware of how the lab relates to other aids and pieces of equipment for teaching, of how this teaching technology relates to methodology and the techniques of instruction, and of how both the foregoing relate to the underlying and supporting disciplines of linguistics, psychology, sociology, education. A teacher with this breadth of perspective can expect to use the lab in the best possible way—or rather in the best possible *ways*, since as yet the language lab is far from having been sufficiently exploited and developed.

The availability of materials, or the need for facilities for producing them
Although the materials commercially available are continually increasing in number, extending in range and improving in quality, few teachers can find more than a fraction of their requirements in the publishers'

lists. This is partly due to the enormous diversity of courses, levels, rates of intensity, target standards and special interests which go to make up the teaching of English. But it is partly also due to the different teaching preferences of individual teachers, or departments, or institutions and also to the fact that materials become dated and lose the freshness of their appeal after a relatively short period. Whatever the reasons, teachers cannot yet expect to be able to purchase all their needs for language lab materials, ready-made from the publishers. Instead they must assume, for the foreseeable future, that a proportion of all their materials will have to be home-made.

In passing, it is worth noticing that the requirement upon teachers that they should have to produce their own materials represents an increased burden on them; no such requirement exists as far as printed books are concerned. Yet there are grounds for arguing that language lab materials require more professional experience and sophistication to produce than is required even to write printed materials, so that language labs must be seen as a very considerable challenge to the teacher, and one which is often not realized until some time after a lab has been installed.

The construction of materials for the language lab is a specialized task; teachers engaged in it for the first time should not underestimate the very great quantity of time and energy that are required in order to do the job well. Until an individual or a team has acquired a good deal of experience it is wise to allow some 300 hours of working time—for planning, drafting, recording, editing, field trials, revisions, re-recording, copying, etc.—in order to produce one single, final hour of classroom material, comprising text and tapes. For fully-integrated audio-visual materials probably 1:500 is a more accurate ratio of final time to preparation time. And of course the teacher embarking upon such a task also needs the basic equipment and facilities for the job.

In other words, to embark upon a serious programme of preparing language lab materials it is necessary to set aside a really large amount of time for the working timetable of highly-skilled teachers. Unless this is done, the lab will not easily be able to build up a collection of suitable materials.

Basic Alternatives in the Design and Use of Language Labs

Design

Many variations exist within the range of possible designs for a language lab. One simple way to distinguish them is to postulate a 'typical' or 'standard' design, and then to indicate 'down-scale' and 'up-scale' alternatives.

The term *language lab* is generally applied to a combination of three essential components, located within a single room or suite of rooms. The essential components are:

(i) a set of specialized tape recording/replay machines, one for each student place, each with a microphone and head-set;

(ii) a communication system linking all the student machines to a central teacher's control panel and providing any of several alternative degrees of inter-communication;

(iii) at each student place, means of giving a measure of acoustic isolation to each learner (normally with a well-padded head-set, but sometimes with a veritable telephone booth for purposes of 'psychological' isolation).

Within this general specification, the various degrees of sophistication centre round the number of functions independently available at each student place, and the degree of central control of those functions that can be exercised by the teacher.

(i) The *typical* lab has recording facilities for each student, as well as a facility for each student to hear either his own efforts, to hear a programme in common with other students, and to converse directly with the teacher.

(ii) The *down-scale* lab has no separate recording facilities at student places and indeed may not use fixed student places at all, as in the 'milking-machine' design.

(iii) The *up-scale* lab has all typical facilities, plus full remote control of each student machine (including fast-forward and fast-rewind) from the control console.

Although the majority of labs use open-spool tape recorders, improvements which have taken place in the quality of sound recording and reproduction using *cassettes* have led to the introduction of this type of recorder in many labs. As long as cassette labs are maintained to a high standard they offer many advantages in convenience of operation, particularly on the part of the student, compared with conventional tape-deck labs.

In the United States there has been available for some years a design of lab in which each student place has a telephone dial, coupled to a switching system and a bank of recorded tapes. The student dials the number of the tape he requires, and then hears it as if it was being played from the teacher's control console. 'Dial-access' systems are available in Europe, also, and they may find a use in very large-scale installations. But it has to be realized that the dial-access system normally presupposes that each student is working on his own rather than as a member of a class, and this raises the question of how the language lab is to be used.

Use

Two alternative systems of use are available:
  (i) as a *specially-equipped classroom*, for simultaneous class-work under the control of the teacher;
  (ii) as a *place for individual work*, in the 'library' mode, with little or no supervision.

These two alternative modes of use are not incompatible, and there is a place for both. Nevertheless, teachers in Europe seem to have increasing reservations about the value of solo work, except in certain specific conditions. As long as the learner is rather sophisticated in his ability to monitor his own efforts, as long as he is well-motivated and diligent, as long as the materials he is using have been skillfuly prepared, and as long as his overall progress is being carefully and continually checked by a teacher, then solo work can be productive and effective. Otherwise many teachers believe that it should be kept down to a very small proportion of the total learning-teaching programme.

Lay-out

In placing the students, some labs retain the 'fore-and-aft' lay-out of the conventional classroom; some teachers prefer a fan-shaped design, perhaps with each successive row tiered above the preceding row, as in a shallow amphitheatre; some teachers on the other hand prefer to avoid any appearance of a normal classroom. When a lab is used only for solo, library-mode work, lay-out is immaterial.

Size

In deciding how many places to provide in a single lab, two main criteria apply. The first is whether the lab will be used as a class: if so, then the size of the lab needs to be related both to the average class size (for obvious organizational reasons) and to the numbers of students that the teaching staff feel able to control under lab conditions. The second criterion might be called the 'sweat-shop effect'. It is technically possible to install hundreds of student places in a single lab—the mythology of language labs contains stories of 'two-hundred-holers' in military language schools—but students tend to become oppressed by the battery-hen atmosphere of any lab that is bigger than a conventional classroom. In practice, most labs in Europe are designed and installed with a capacity of between 15 and 30 places.

Materials

As with any branch of teaching, the preparation of materials offers scope for ingenuity, innovation and imagination. Language lab materials were characterized, for a long period, by surpassing dullness, close similarity of one course to all others and narrowness of range in what was attempted. Many teachers whose experience of language lab teaching has been unhappy owe the fact to poor materials. Yet the potentialities of lab materials are very great; as enterprising teachers experiment with fresh techniques and pass on their results to other teachers it gradually becomes clear that the language lab can be used in effective and enjoyable ways for the teaching—or at least for *supporting* the teaching—of almost every aspect of language. (Even the teaching of reading can be assisted by listening to the recording of a text while simultaneously reading the written version.)

The Methodological Role of the Lab

The distinction made in the preceding paragraph between *teaching* with the lab and *supporting teaching* with the lab relates to the methodological role or function which most teachers ascribe to the lab. Exception must be made of the special (and rather rare) conditions, noted earlier, in which individual language work can be made effective. In all normal circumstances the language lab is regarded as being unsuitable for initial presentation and best employed in close integration with the total teaching programme.

Some teachers incorporate lab work as one hour in four, or a maximum of one hour in five, as in the following 'module':

Hour 1: new material presented in normal class.

2: follow-up (under the teacher) in lab.

3: work in small groups (not in the lab).

4: follow-up in normal class.

5: further consolidation, working alone in lab.

Conclusions

After more than fifteen years of language lab use a number of general conclusions have become obvious. The first is that language labs cannot of themselves teach anything. Second, it is just as easy to teach badly or ineffectively with a language lab as without one. Thirdly, once a lab has been successfully incorporated into the teaching, the range of possibilities for extending its use are very great: given a sound professional basis, sufficient time and plenty of enthusiasm, a language lab can be made into a source of variety and wit in teaching, and can deserve its place as a normal (though expensive) part of the equipment of the language teacher.

14 Where has all the money gone? The need for cost-effectiveness studies in the teaching of foreign languages

Behind the term 'applied linguistics', both as it is used in this book and as it was used at the First International Congress on Applied Linguistics at Nancy in 1964, is a general agreement that the study and teaching of languages can benefit in important ways from the rigorous theoretical approach of modern studies in linguistics, in psychology and in learning theory, as well as from the results of recent and current research in these disciplines. It is agreed, too, that the best of instructional procedures, the methodology of teaching (or, if you prefer, techniques for facilitating learning), continue to be central to language teaching; and that these techniques can be very greatly improved by the use of appropriate aids and equipment, which range from the gramophone through language laboratories and closed-circuit television to computer-assisted learning.

Until some eight years ago the teaching of foreign languages was a 'chalk and talk' profession, in which the only necessary expenditure was on a teacher and a textbook—i.e. the minimum expense, below which organized instruction barely exists. Nowadays foreign language teaching is accepted as being a profession in which large and increasing sums of money (mostly *public* money, we should notice) are spent on aids and equipment: especially but not exclusively on language laboratories, on which alone it is estimated that over a million pounds has been spent in Britain in the past five years.

These very large extra costs are facts, even if the precise amounts are not known. What observable changes have occurred in the output of the system—i.e. in the foreign language achievement of the boys, girls and adults who have been taught—which can be plausibly attributed to this additional expenditure? Is there in fact *any* change? If so, how can it be measured? What monetary value can be put upon it? Does the present system of examinations, canonized long before this expenditure was contemplated, provide a useful index of changes in output? If not, should not some alternative assessment be devised, so that some kind of feedback exists from the learners, who are the output of the system, to the teachers and others who operate it?

A profession which values rigour in its outlook should ask such questions: but even if it does not they are likely to be asked from outside the profession. Already administrators are beginning to ask questions which seem to them necessary in order to justify the now sizeable expenditure on aids and equipment for language teaching. This money has to compete with many other claims. There are signs already that the honeymoon is over: where once claims were met with little demur (or even where teachers found language labs thrust upon them by administrative decision, regardless of whether their teaching situation warranted it) now such questions are being asked as this: 'What value can be placed on the improved results of language teaching using aids and equipment, to set against the money you have spent?'

There are at least four obvious replies to such questions.

(i) The techniques of cost-effectiveness analysis have never been applied by economists to language teaching, so that no factual answer is available.

(ii) The aims of language teaching are rapidly changing, and consequently the end-product of the system is changing, so that there is no firm basis for comparison and evaluation.

(iii) The use of aids and equipment is part of the 'style of learning' of the 1960's and 1970's: the customers and their parents expect them to be used, and if they are not the institution concerned suffers a drop in recruitment, a loss of reputation, a reduction of confidence ('I shouldn't send Johnnie to that school—they haven't even got a language lab') so that in this sense the need for expenditure on equipment is determined by criteria unrelated to the effectiveness of teaching.

(iv) The long-term effects of the new-style teaching can be expected to improve both the standards of the pupils and the expectations of the public, thus rendering such bureaucratic questions unnecessary.

But of course these replies are quite inadequate. If cost-effectiveness studies have not been done yet they should be commissioned now; techniques do exist for evaluating changes in aims and standards; the expectations of the pupils and the public do not alter the fact that massive expenditure has actually taken place; the probable long-term effects are no excuse for not examining the current situation. Sophisticated techniques and procedures for such studies already exist within the discipline of economics; all that an applied linguist can do is to indicate a few of the main lines along which such a study might proceed.

A study of cost-effectiveness entails the analysis of the costs arising from various decisions, in relation to the benefits resulting from these decisions. To do this it becomes essential to know what is included under the heading of costs and what under benefits, and the degree of causality between them.

Studies of this kind are of course studies of a system. There is little to be gained from attempting such studies at the level of a single school, college or university department. What is being attempted is the measurement and quantification of those changes in the output of the system which can be attributed to expenditure on particular parts of the system. It is essential to take account of all relevant parts of the system. Thus it is not simply the cost of purchasing language labs that has to be considered, but also the cost of such other factors as: giving further training to teachers; the adaptation of classrooms; the monopolizing of a large classroom by a single subject; the employment of lab stewards or technicians; the time spent by teaching staff on the preparation of materials; and a great many others.

Costs include (a) sums of money expended as the result of a particular decision, and (b) any reduction in benefits that may accrue. Taking costs first, these may involve at least three kinds of expenditure:

  (i) *Capital expenditure* on aids and equipment and possibly on accommodation to house them, not forgetting charges for interest, depreciation and provision for replacement, items which between them can very considerably inflate an apparently modest capital outlay.

  (ii) *Recurrent expenditure*, including the salaries of any teachers who would otherwise not be employed, the cost of any special components introduced in the initial training of teachers, the cost of vacation courses or other in-service training, the running costs of equipment, costs of maintenance, the wages of technicians, the cost of special books or software in connection with the proper running of the equipment, etc.

  (iii) *Expenditure on research and development* where this is directly related to the introduction and use of new aids and equipment. (Here it is arguable that some at least of such expenditure should be allocated against costs but should be separately charged.)

The negative aspect of costs, namely reduction in benefits, might conceivably include the case where a highly paid teacher makes a considerable reduction in his classroom teaching time when he takes over responsibility for organizing a large language lab installation: cost-effectiveness studies might well indicate whether or not it would be cheaper to employ additional, lower-paid supervisory staff in order to avoid the loss of the expensive services of a specialist teacher.

Benefits have at least two aspects: improvements in the value of the end-product of the system, and reductions in real costs. The first of these, improvements in the value of the end-product, it is difficult to set a monetary figure on, but it represents nevertheless an important component of the system. For instance, if a given force of teachers customarily processes up to the average level of competence 1,000 pupils in five years, and if after the expenditure of £100,000 on aids, equipment and supporting costs the same force of teachers in the subsequent five years turns out 1,200 pupils, that represents an improvement of some 20% in the value of the end-product. But most of the effects of expenditure on aids and equipment are likely to be less clear-cut, and to centre on changes in the quality of the product, and therefore on changes in its value. The remark 'Johnny speaks better French than his older brother did' may in fact point to a basis for an assessment, as long as a plausible figure for the value of Johnny's French in comparison with that of his brother (say, a 15% improvement) can be postulated to represent the real improvement in the product. The other aspect of benefits, namely the reduction of costs, occurs if a given target is reached in fewer hours of teaching, for example; it can also occur if it can be shown that some of the time previously spent in 'learning' was concerned with irrelevances, so that former waste of time is now reduced; or if the same number of pupils is processed by a smaller and cheaper teaching force.

A cost-effectiveness analysis need not be concerned solely with the costs and benefits of specific decisions or particular kinds of expenditure. It can and perhaps should be used to answer also the other obvious administrator's questions, as to whether the existing financial investment in language teaching is giving maximum benefits, and whether better use could not be made of our existing resources.

This aspect of our operations would be likely to give rise on investigation to doubts on two counts: first, on whether more could not be done to reduce wastage, and second, on whether we could not increase our productivity per unit cost. We are open to considerable criticism over the question of wastage in language teaching. Let us take two examples. Large numbers of pupils still fail language exams at O-levels and thereafter take their language studies no further. If one regards the monetary value of the level of achievement represented by a fail at O-level as being effectively equal to zero, then every year a sizeable percentage of the total products of the school language teaching system, upon whom hundreds of hours of expensive teaching have been expended, has to be written off. Many people would extend this very low value to include also those who achieve a bare pass at O-level, in which case the wastage rate at the end of the biggest single production stage of the system might be regarded as disturbingly high. The second example is less obvious, but still may warrant some thought. It is common in some university departments of modern languages to admit to a first year of studies a very large number of students, but to fail a high percentage of them at the end of the first year. In their case, too, they may be regarded as wastage in terms of the productivity of the system, since much expensive labour has been allocated to teaching many students who do not become adequately-valued products of the system, while the value of the labour applied to teaching those who will be successful has been diluted by the presence of the future drop-outs. Since entry requirements to these courses are already very high, the case is not on all fours with that of the O-level failures. In particular it may be argued that A-level exam results do not identify the top $x\%$ of entrants, who alone are the ones capable of taking an honours degree, and that therefore the first year acts as a necessary filter. This may be true, or it may be that better selection procedures could be devised and operated at lower cost and therefore with benefit to the department concerned and the system as a whole. Clearly there is much to be investigated in the profession, in terms of wastage. It could well emerge that we would be wise to divert some money and effort to the improvement of selection procedures for entry to language courses at various levels, to the avoidance of a high drop-out rate, to the improvement of motivation among those who start language courses, and perhaps above all to avoiding the situation where the terminal standard reached by a sizeable proportion of learners is generally felt to be of virtually no value.

Increasing our productivity per unit cost entails asking whether the training of teachers is adequately geared to the changing aims and techniques of the profession; whether teachers once trained are made use of in the most effective way; whether the syllabuses, textbooks and other course materials are geared to aims and techniques appropriate to the equipment which has been purchased (or whether perhaps there may not be in some places language labs acting as façades for continuing the grammar-grind); whether the evaluation procedures—the examinations—determine the teaching, and if so, whether the examinations are appropriate to teaching as best carried out using aids and equipment. It is widely agreed that these kinds of 'impedance mis-match'—between aims and materials, and between methods and exams—are economically wasteful and therefore constitute a point where improvements in productivity might be made.

In other sectors of education where cost-effectiveness studies have been attempted it has been suggested that the unit costs per student are dramatically reduced once full use is made of the techniques of programmed learning. This is an area where relatively little progress has been made in foreign language teaching, although there are a number of American programmes, chiefly in the field of pronunciation teaching. There are good reasons for the slow rate of progress: learning languages turns out to entail a number of different kinds of learning and many different kinds of practice; for most of them, the only suitable monitoring device seems to be the trained teacher. Nevertheless there are surely some points within the total system where the introduction of programmed learning could be attempted. One thinks, for example, of the remarkable programmed, self-instructional Teacher Education Program of English Language Services, designed to train overseas students how to teach, and how to teach an English course. The degree of success of the prototype suggests that here is one point, teacher training, where substantial savings might be made by the introduction of programmed learning. There are almost certainly several others.

One of the most difficult areas of any cost-effectiveness study is likely to be the assessment of the change in value of the products of the system as a result of changes in aims. Suppose the aim of teaching language L at school, for example, is that those successful at A-level should be well-versed in the literature of language L, with only 10% or less of their total assessment allocated to an evaluation of their command of the spoken language. A successful pupil might be assessed at a value to the system of 100. Now suppose the aims change, and command of the spoken language becomes very much more important, and suppose this change is in fact reflected in the teaching. What is now the value of the successful A-level pupil? Perhaps in the ideal case we might assess him at 125. But if the examination remains unchanged, how do we know how far the pupil satisfies the new aims? An examination cannot simultaneously and equally well assess pupils in relation to two different sets of criteria. The question is raised here not in order to provide an answer but in order to suggest that out of a cost-effectiveness study there may come observations with painful or unwelcome consequences for the present system, and especially for our system of examinations.

A study of cost-effectiveness in the teaching of foreign languages (which one hopes would include English as a foreign language) is urgently needed. Given the present level of total expenditure on language teaching over the world as a whole, which must run at scores of millions of pounds per year, an overall gain of even a fraction of 1% would be a sizeable advance. A study would have to be a joint enterprise, with specialists in economics working beside others widely experienced in the language teaching profession. The aims of such a study might be two in number: (1) to determine the results in terms of cost-effectiveness of the introduction of new aims, methods and equipment in the teaching of foreign languages; and (2) to enquire into the extent to which existing resources are effectively deployed and into any means by which productivity per student cost in foreign language teaching could be improved. If the profession can set up a study of this kind, it would be justifying in respect of its own operations the insistence upon rigour which is one of the major features of applied linguistics.

Bibliography

These pages include all the works referred to in the text, together with a number of sources of primary reference and further reading.

ABERCROMBIE, D. *Problems and Principles*, Longman, 1956
—— *Elements of General Phonetics*, Edinburgh University Press, 1967
ALLEN, J. P. B. and CORDER, S. P. (eds.) *The Edinburgh Course in Applied Linguistics* Volume 1: *Readings for Applied Linguistics*. Volume 2: *Papers in Applied Linguistics*. Volume 3: *Techniques in Applied Linguistics*. Volume 4: *Testing and Experimental Methods*. Oxford University Press, 1973–77.
ANDERSSON, T. 'Children's Learning of a Second Language: another view', *Modern Language Journal*, Volume 57, 1973
ANTHONY, E. M. 'Approach, Method and Technique'. In H. Allen and R. Campbell (eds.), *Teaching English as a Second Language*, McGraw-Hill, 1972
BAR-ADON, A. and LEOPOLD, W. F. (eds.) *Child Language: A Book of Readings*, Prentice-Hall, 1971
BEEBY, C. E. *The Quality of Education in Developing Countries*, Harvard University Press, 1966
BENNETT, W. A. *Applied Linguistics and Language Learning*, Hutchinson, 1974
BENSON, J. D. and GREAVES, W. S. *The Language People Really Use*, Book Society of Canada, 1973
BERNSTEIN, B. 'Elaborated and Restricted Codes'. In S. Lieberson (ed.), *Explorations in Sociolinguistics*, Bloomington, Indiana, 1967
—— 'A Sociolinguistic approach to social learning', in F. Williams (ed.), *Language and Poverty*, Markham, 1970
BILLOWS, L. *Techniques of Language Teaching*, Longman, 1961
BRIGHT, J. A. and McGREGOR, G. P. *Teaching English as a Second Language*, Longman, 1970
BROWN, R. *A First Language: The Early Stages*, Allen and Unwin, 1973
BRUNER, J. *Toward a Theory of Instruction*, Belknap Press, 1971
CANDLIN, C. 'The Status of Pedagogical Grammars'. In S. P. Corder and E. Roulet (eds.), *Theoretical Linguistic models in Applied Linguistics*, AIMAV and Didier, 1973
CARROLL, J. B. 'The Contribution of Psychological Theory and Educa-

Bibliography 173

tional Research to the Teaching of Foreign Languages'. In A. Valdman (ed.) *Trends in Language Teaching*, McGraw-Hill, 1966

CASHDAN, A. et al (eds.) *Language in Education: A Source Book*, Routledge and Kegan Paul, 1972

CATFORD, J. C. *A Linguistic Theory of Translation*, Oxford University Press, 1965

CHOMSKY, N. *Language and Mind*, Harcourt Brace, 1972

CORDER, S. P. *Introducing Applied Linguistics*, Penguin, 1973

COWIE, A. P. and MACKIN, R. *The Oxford Dictionary of Current Idiomatic English. Vol 1: Verbs with Prepositions and Particles*, Oxford University Press, 1975

CURRIE, W. B. *New Directions in Teaching English Language*, Longman, 1973

DICKINSON, L. and MACKIN, R. *Varieties of Spoken English*, Oxford University Press, 1966

DILLARD, J. L. *Black English*, Random House, 1972

DILLER, K. *Generative Grammar, Structural Linguistics, and Language Teaching*, Newbury House, 1971

DOUGHTY, P., PEARCE, J. and THORNTON, G. *Language in Use*, Edward Arnold, 1971

—— *Exploring Language*, Edward Arnold, 1972

DYKSTRA, G. 'Today's Curriculum for Tomorrow's World', Monograph of the Hawaii Association for Supervision and Curriculum Development, 1970

ENGLISH TEACHING INFORMATION CENTRE *English for Academic Study, with special reference to Science and Technology*, The British Council, 1975

FIRTH, J. R. *Papers in Linguistics*, Oxford University Press, 1957.

FRENCH, F. G. *The Teaching of English Abroad*, 3 volumes, Oxford University Press, 1948

FRIES, C. C. *Teaching and Learning English as a Foreign Language*, University of Michigan Press, 1947

FRISBY, A. W. *Teaching English*, Longman, 1957

GIGLIOLI, P. P. *Language and Social Context*, Penguin, 1972

GIMSON, A. C. *An Introduction to the Pronunciation of English*, Edward Arnold, 1962

GIRARD, D. *Linguistics and Foreign Language Teaching*, Longman, 1972

GOUIN, F. *The Art of Teaching and Studying Languages*, G. Phillip, 1892

GREGORY, M. 'Aspects of Varieties Differentiation', *Journal of Linguistics*, Volume 3, No. 2, 1967

HALLIDAY, M. A. K., MCINTOSH, A. and STREVENS, P. *The Linguistic Sciences and Language Teaching*, Longman, 1964

HALLIDAY, M. A. K. *Explorations in the Functions of Language*, Edward Arnold, 1973

—— *Learning How to Mean*, Edward Arnold, 1975

HAUGEN, E. and BLOOMFIELD, M. (eds.) *Language As A Human Problem*, Lutterworth Press, 1974

HAYES, A. S. *Language Laboratory Facilities*, Oxford University Press, 1968

HORNBY, A. S. *The Teaching of Structural Words and Sentence Patterns*, 3 volumes, Oxford University Press, 1973
—— *A Guide to Patterns and Usage in English*, (2nd edition), Oxford University Press, 1975
—— *Oxford Advanced Learner's Dictionary of Current English*, Oxford University Press, 1975
HUXLEY, R. and INGRAM, E. (eds.) *Language Acquisition: Models and Methods*, Academic Press, 1971
HYMES, D. 'Towards Ethnographies of Communication: The Analysis of Communicative Events'. In P. P. Giglioli, *Language and Social Context*, Penguin, 1972
INGRAM, E. 'Psychology and Language Learning'. In J. P. B. Allen and S. P. Corder, *The Edinburgh Course in Applied Linguistics*, Oxford University Press, 1974
ISAACS, N. *The Growth of Understanding in The Young Child: a Brief Introduction to Piaget's Work*, Ward Lock Educational Company, 1961
JAKOBOVITS, L. *Foreign Language Learning: a Psycholinguistic Analysis of the Issues*, Newbury House, 1970
JESPERSEN, O. *How to Teach a Foreign Language*, Allen and Unwin, 1904
JOHNSON, F. C. *English as a Second Language: An Individualized Approach*, Jacaranda Press, 1973. John Murray, 1974
JOHNSON, F. C. and PAULSTON, C. B. *Individualising the Language Classroom*, Boston, 1976
JONES, D. *An Outline of English Phonetics*, Heffer, 1956
—— *The Phoneme*, Heffer, 1962
JOOS, M. *The Five Clocks*, Harcourt Brace, 1967
KACHRU, B. 'The Indianness in Indian English', *Word* Volume 21, 1965
—— 'Models of English for the Third World: White Man's Linguistic Burden or Language Pragmatics?', *TESOL Quarterly*, Volume 10, No. 2, 1976
KELLY, L. G. *25 Centuries of Language Teaching*, Newbury House, 1969
LADO, R. *Language Teaching: A Scientific Approach*, McGraw-Hill, 1964
LAWTON, D. *Social Class, Language and Education*, Routledge and Kegan Paul, 1968
LEE, W. R. 'What type of syllabus for the teaching of English as a second or foreign language?', *International Review of Applied Linguistics* (forthcoming)
—— 'For and against an early start', *Foreign Language Annals* (forthcoming)
LEECH, G. and SVARTVIK, J. *A Communicative Grammar of English*, Longman, 1975
LENNEBERG, E. and E. (eds.) *Foundations of Language Development: a Multidisciplinary Approach*, 2 volumes, Academic Press, 1974
LOVELL, K. *Educational Psychology and Children*, University of London Press, 1973
MACKEY, W. F. *Language Teaching Analysis*, Longman, 1965
McGREGOR, G. P. *English in Africa*, Heinemann Educational Books, 1971

MACNAMARA, J. 'Nurseries, Streets and Classrooms: Some Comparisons and Deductions'. *Modern Language Journal*, Volume 57, 1973

MARCKWARDT, A. *American English*, Oxford University Press, 1958

MARCKWARDT, A. and QUIRK, R. *A Common Language: British and American English*, BBC and Voice of America, 1967

MENCKEN, H. L. *The American Language*, Routledge and Kegan Paul, 1967

O'CONNOR, J. D. and ARNOLD, G. F. *The Intonation of Colloquial English*, Longman, 1961

PALMER, H. E. *The Principles of Language Study*, Oxford University Press, 1964

—— *The Scientific Study and Teaching of Languages*, Oxford University Press, 1964

PERREN, G. (ed.) *Teachers of English as a Second Language: Their Training and Preparation*, Cambridge University Press, 1968

PERREN, G. and TRIM, J. L. (eds.) *Applications of Linguistics: Selected Papers of the Second International Congress of Applied Linguistics*, Cambridge University Press, 1971

PIAGET, J. *The Psychology of Intelligence*, Routledge and Kegan Paul, 1950

PIAGET J. and SZEMINSKA, A. *The Child's Conception of Number*, Routledge and Kegan Paul, 1952

PIAGET, J. *Logic and Psychology*, Manchester University Press, 1953. Basic Books, 1957

—— *The Language and Thought of the Child*, Routledge and Kegan Paul, 1959

QUIRK, R. and SMITH, A. H. (eds.) *The Teaching of English*, Secker and Warburg, 1959, Oxford University Press, 1964

QUIRK, R., GREENBAUM, S., LEECH G. *A Grammar of Contemporary English*, Longman 1972

QUIRK, R. and GREENBAUM, S. *A University Grammar of English*, Longman, 1973

RICHARDSON, M. *Writing and Writing Patterns*, University of London Press, 1935

RIVERS, W. M. *The Psychologist and the Foreign Language Teacher*, University of Chicago Press, 1964

—— *Teaching Foreign Language Skills*, University of Chicago Press, 1968

ROULET, E. *Théories Grammaticales, Descriptions et Enseignement des Langues*, Longman, 1975

SADLER, J. E. (ed.) *Comenius*, Collier Macmillan, 1969

SINCLAIR, J. McH. *A Course in Spoken Language: Grammar*, Oxford University Press, 1972

SINCLAIR, J. McH. and COULTHARD, R. M. *Towards an Analysis of Discourse: The English Used by Teachers and Pupils*, Oxford University Press, 1975

SPENCER, J. (ed.) *Language in Africa*, Cambridge University Press, 1963

SPOLSKY, B., GREEN, J. B. and READ, J. *A Model for the Description, Analysis and Perhaps Evaluation of Bilingual Education*, Navajo Reading Study Progress Report No. 23, Albuquerque, 1974

STACK, E. M. *The Language Laboratory and Modern Language Teaching*, Oxford University Press, 1971

STERN, H. H. *Foreign Languages in Primary Education*, Oxford University Press, 1967

—— *Languages and the Young School Child*, Oxford University Press, 1969

—— *Perspectives on Second Language Teaching*, Ontario Institute for Studies in Education, 1970

STODDART, J. and F. *The Teaching of English to Immigrant Children*, University of London Press, 1968

STREVENS, P. *British and American English*, Collier Macmillan, 1972

—— 'Technical, Technological and Scientific English', *English Language Teaching Journal*, Volume 27, No. 3, 1973

—— 'Problems of Learning and Teaching Science through a Foreign Language', *Studies in Science Education*, Volume 3, University of Leeds, 1976

—— 'English as an International Language: local forms of English and their suitability as a model for EFL', *ELT Documents*, 1977 (forthcoming)

—— 'English for Special Purposes: a perspective and an analysis', *Studies in Language Learning*, Urbana, Illinois (forthcoming)

SWEET, H. *The Practical Study of Languages*, Oxford University Press, 1964

TONGUE, R. *The English of Singapore and Malaysia*, Eastern Universities Press, 1974

TRIM, J. L. 'Modern Languages in Education, with special reference to a projected European unit/credit system', Council of Europe EES Symposium 57,3, 1973

—— 'A unit/credit scheme for adult language learning.' In G. Perren (ed.), *Teaching Languages to Adults for Special Purposes*, CILT Reports and Papers, No. 11, 1974.

VALDMAN, A. (ed.) *Trends in Language Teaching*, McGraw-Hill, 1966

VALETTE, R. M. and DISICK, R. S. *Modern Language Performance Objectives and Individualization*, Harcourt Brace, 1972

VAN EK, J. *The Threshold Level in a Unit/Credit System for Modern Language Learning by Adults*, Council of Europe, 1975

WARDHAUGH, R. 'TESOL: Current Problems and Language Practices'. In H. Allen and R. Campbell (eds.) *Teaching English as a Second Language*, McGraw-Hill, 1972

WEST, M. *Learning to Read a Foreign Language*, Longman, 1955

—— *Teaching English in Difficult Circumstances*, Longman, 1960

WHITE, R. V. 'The Language, the Learner and the Syllabus', *Regional English Language Centre Journal*, Volume 6, No. 1, 1975

WILKINS, D., *Linguistics in Language Teaching*, Edward Arnold, 1972

—— *Notional Syllabuses: a Contribution to Foreign Language Curriculum Development*, Oxford University Press, 1976

WINDSOR-LEWIS, J. *A Concise Pronouncing Dictionary of British and American English*, Oxford University Press, 1972

Professional Journals and Periodicals

There are a large number of professional journals and periodicals, many of them regional in their scope or intended for members of a particular organization. The following is a selected list of some of those which from time to time carry articles along the general lines reflected in this book.

BBC Modern English   10 issues per year
8 Hainton Avenue,
Grimsby,
South Humberside DN32 9 BB

ELT Documents   4 issues per year
English Teaching Information Centre,
The British Council,
10 Spring Gardens,
London SW1A 2BN

English Language Teaching Journal   4 issues per year
Oxford University Press,
Press Road,
Neasden,
London N.W.10

English Teaching Forum   2 or 3 issues per
1750 Pennsylvania Avenue,   year
Washington DC,
U.S.A.

Language Learning   2 issues per year
2001 North University Building,
University of Michigan,
Ann Arbor,
Michigan 48104,
U.S.A.

Language-Teaching Abstracts   4 issues per year
P.O. Box 22206,
San Diego,
California 92122

Modern English Teacher   3 issues per year
8 Hainton Avenue,
Grimsby,
South Humberside DN32 9BB

RELC Journal   2 issues per year
Regional English Language Centre,
30 Orange Grove Road,
Singapore 6

TESOL Quarterly   4 issues per year
455 Nevils Building,
Georgetown University,
Washington DC 20057
U.S.A.

Index

Abercrombie, D., 130
accent, 65, 75, 122, **134–9**, 146, 151,
153, 154, 156
achievement
constraints on, 14, 28–31
failure of, 10, 169
in FL learning, 166
standards in pronunciation, 86
time /achievement relationship, 29
acquisition, 13, 41, 46, 48, 50, 121
contrasted with learning a foreign
language, 13
of mother tongue by infant, 41, 50,
66, 75
administration of language teaching,
14, 15, 31
administrative apparatus, 17
possibly counterproductive, 50
adolescents, 10, 17, 18
learning pronunciation, 83
adults, 17
learning pronunciation, 82, 83
advanced stage, 19, 116
definition, 114
readers for, 116
aids and equipment
cost-effectiveness, **166–71**
elements in applied linguistics, 39
aims, 14, 15, 167
educational, 17, 19
need to specify, 10
special purposes, 19
targets of achievement, 59, 65
American English, 132, **147–56**
applied linguistics, 16, 22, 51, 77, 80,
166, 167, 171
definition, 37–40
approach, 4, 11, 13, 21, 23, 27, 129, 130
American and British contrasted, 55
definition, 23

flexibility of, 62
assessment (see evaluation)
audio-lingual method, 3, 5, 8, 10, 23
audio-visual method, 4

'BBC English', 139
Booby, C. E., 26
beginner stage, 17, 114-15
definition, 113
Bernstein, B., 49
elaborated and restricted codes, 122
Bloomfieldian linguistics, 3, 8, 9, 16,
57, 65
British English, 132, **147–56**
Bruner, J., 66
Burt, C., 66

Canadian English, 11
Canadian French, 11
Candlin, C., 12
Carroll, J. B., 5
categories
communicative, 107
functional, 64, 107
notional, 25, 61, 64, 107
Catford, J. C., 28, 130
Chomsky, N., 9, 59 (see transformational-generative theory)
class
varieties relating to, 131, 135, 136
codes, elaborated and restricted, 122
coding, decoding, contrasted with
deciphering, 112
cognitive-code teaching, 5, 6, 23
Comenius, 26
communicative
abilities, 26, 61, 66
categories, **107**
command, 60
competence, 121
objectives, 7

180 Index

WITHDRAWN